MACMILLAN STUDIES I
MANAGEM

C000081502

This series is designed to fill the n
of major aspects of marketing ma
essentially upon European institutio.
to suggest that experience and practice in other aavan...
will be ignored, but rather that the treatment will reflect European
custom and attitudes as opposed to American, which have tended
to dominate so much of the marketing literature.

Each volume is the work of an acknowledged authority on that
subject and combines a distillation of the best and most up-to-date
research findings with a clear statement of their relevance to im-
proved managerial practice. A concise style is followed throughout,
and extensive use is made of summaries, check-lists and references to
related work. Thus each work may be viewed as both an introduction to and a reference work on its particular subject. Further,
while each book is self-contained, the series as a whole comprises a
handbook of marketing management.

The series is designed for both students and practitioners of
marketing. Lecturers will find the treatment adequate as the foun-
dation for in-depth study of each topic by more advanced students
who have already pursued an introductory and broadly based course
in marketing. Similarly, managers will find each book to be both
a useful *aide-mémoire* and a reference source.

MACMILLAN STUDIES IN MARKETING MANAGEMENT

General Editor: Professor Michael J. Baker
University of Strathclyde

PUBLISHED TITLES

Organisational Buying Behaviour	Roy W. Hill and Terry J. Hillier
A Management Guide to Market Research	James M. Livingstone
International Marketing Management	James M. Livingstone
Pricing	F. Livesey
Marketing: Theory and Practice	Professor Michael J. Baker (editor)
Product Policy and Management	Professor Michael J. Baker and Ronald McTavish

FORTHCOMING

Public Relations in Marketing Management	Frank Jefkins

INTERNATIONAL MARKETING MANAGEMENT

James M. Livingstone

First edition 1976
Reprinted 1978

Published by
THE MACMILLAN PRESS LTD
London and Basingstoke
Associated companies in Delhi Dublin
Hong Kong Johannesburg Lagos Melbourne
New York Singapore and Tokyo

ISBN 0 333 19237 0

Printed in Hong Kong

Contents

PART II   THE PROCESS OF EXPORTING

Preface

This book is intended for the executive and the potential executive. It is therefore about policy rather than commercial practice. In many small firms both policy decisions and their detailed execution are the responsibility of one person; but it is with this individual in his policy-deciding role that the book is concerned.

Part I deals with the general background upon which a decision to export is based, including a general analysis of the problems of exporting. Part II is perhaps most conventional in its approach in that it deals with the mechanics – not as a substitute for a book on general commercial or legal practice – but to suggest to the relative newcomer to exporting some of the decisions he will have to make, as well as the sources of aid which are available.

Part III of the book considers in outline some of the problems of 'going international' in the sense of moving from the role of exporting to actually manufacturing and distributing from overseas bases. The multinational company faces completely different problems from the purely exporting company; but the logic of much postwar development points to the increasing importance of this kind of marketing. Many firms which are merely contemplating a venture into overseas marketing may find that, within a decade or two, logic and the pursuit of profits will carry them further along the multinational road than they now envisage.

1975   J. M. L.

Part I
The Issues in Exporting

The first part of this book is concerned with some of the basic issues of exporting – the circumstances under which it may prove profitable, general characteristics of overseas markets and the alternative methods of trading available.

A decision to export or not to export has many implications for the future growth or even survival of many firms. Most firms which do go in for exporting enjoy some measure of success, and for some, in retrospect, it is the single policy decision which transformed their prospects. But it is still only too easy for other firms to stumble into important policy decisions, largely by dealing with problems as and when they arise, even in circumstances where these might readily have been foreseen.

Thus, for example, the three most important initial decisions are what, where and how to export. All three are often taken on an intuitive basis, although these decisions are likely to have very long-term consequences.

It is impossible in a book of this small compass to suggest a magic formula which will resolve the problems, but at least it is possible to suggest that some of the decisions which are taken most casually, because they do not involve immediate financial risk, may have these far-reaching implications, and therefore deserve rather more care than they are sometimes given.

Part I

The Issues in Exporting

Chapter 1

The Pros and Cons of Exporting

INTRODUCTION

The importance of exporting is so obvious as to require little reiteration. It is, however, an awkward fact that most of the arguments which spring most readily to mind apply to the national not the company interest. The first task of this chapter is therefore to argue that in many instances, even where exporting is seen at best as a marginal activity which can be dropped or cut as and when the home market absorbs output, the true interests of the company may be inadequately understood. Exporting increasingly may be a necessary condition for a secure home market.

Given that the role of exporting on a company's development may be underestimated, there is often a profound difference between marketing at home and overseas, and this difference is ignored at peril. The marked public and official approval of exporting has to be balanced against the ill-understood problems which can arise in a foreign market. This chapter, in very broad terms, attempts to sketch out the issues which affect the exporter.

WHY EXPORT?

Replying that it is in the *national* interest for a firm to enter the export market does not mean that it is in the *firm's* interest to do so. If a firm can make its profits more easily by selling at home rather than overseas then it may be entirely rational in concentrating on the home market. Accusations of unpatriotic behaviour are not likely to cut much ice – and probably rightly so.

Two dubious arguments in favour of exporting are sometimes advanced. The first of these, 'Exporting is fun' (a proposition put forward by a former British Prime Minister), needs qualification. Exporting can be an *adventure*, in the sense that it poses new problems against an unfamiliar background with risk of heavy loss; whether this constitutes fun depends on one's sense of humour. To approach the problems of exporting light-heartedly is to court certain trouble. The second argument, that exporting is patriotic, contains the elements of a dangerous fallacy. Some firms export knowing that profit margins are going to be a good deal less than in the home market; and they do a perfectly good job. But an appeal to patriotism can lead to dangerous attitudes. The most pernicious development may arise from an idea that the firm is doing a favour to the government. This becomes translated into the idea that it is doing a favour to the overseas buyer. A sense that the customer is somehow being favoured by the exporter is frankly disastrous. It can lead to indifferent attention to the customer's requirements, poor after-sales servicing and a tendency to place the interest of the more important clients (i.e. the more profitable domestic consumers) ahead of those of the new-found overseas customers with a consequent deterioration of relations with the latter, a situation which would not have arisen had the relationship started on a more realistic basis. Even where export marketing is not *so* profitable as home marketing, it should still be a sound economic proposition; a supplement to, rather than an alternative to, home marketing. When exporting causes a loss, then no justification in terms of a warm glow of patriotism can be sustained.

A second danger inherent in patriotic exporting is that of enthusiasm followed by disillusion. It is one thing to be patriotic when patriotism is exciting, if not always rewarding; it is another when things begin to go wrong. Firms which have been beguiled into exporting have sometimes found themselves facing problems caused by inadequate preparation and forward planning. They have committed the sort of cardinal errors in marketing which they would never dream of committing in the home market. In time they may recover from their mistakes. In some cases, having sustained heavy losses apparently in the cause of patriotism (and not, if the truth were faced, through their marketing policies), they retire from the scene disgruntled and unwilling to investigate more hopeful markets. By itself this sort of experience is unfortunate for the firm. In fact the ill-effects can go a good deal further, particularly if their products are the sort that need after-sales service. For the chances are that the marketing effort will have had some success; someone overseas laid out money on a product, only to find that the expected servicing facilities were subsequently withdrawn. Not only has the original exporting firm lost money for itself by its ill-advised and ill-prepared foray, it may have lost money for its customers overseas and created national prejudice against other British firms which will take a long time to die down.

Patriotic exporting too in a number of firms tends to burn brightest in recession conditions or when there is a credit squeeze at home. This is not surprising since credit squeezes, whether or not they are successful, are intended among other things to encourage firms to sell overseas. Firms which will sell overseas in an emergency (and a tight home market is their definition of an emergency), will be equally ready to pull out as soon as the home market begins to expand; again creating ill will overseas. If challenged on the policy, they may reply with a fair degree of plausibility and self-conviction that their experience of the overseas market showed low-profit margins and that they owed a duty to their shareholders and staff to concentrate on the more profitable domestic market. There is an element of self-fulfilling prophecy in this situation. If a firm thinks of export marketing as a short-term proposition in an emergency, where a breakeven in costs and revenue has to come quickly or not at all, it will be reluctant to spend any more than is absolutely necessary in promoting exports by maintaining stocks and servicing facilities for overseas markets. Following such a policy, the firm may be unable to recognise any long-term prospects worth exploiting and worth ploughing more resources into. Lack of forward planning ensures only a short-term marketing policy. This policy, in turn, brings about exactly the sort of results which had been anticipated on what was originally an inadequate analysis of the situation.

If export marketing is seen as a marginal and transient activity there is a reluctance to adapt to the conditions most acceptable to the overseas market. One of the themes of this book will be the difficulties which can arise from a too ready acceptance of the notion that what is normal in the home market can be taken for granted as equally normal in the overseas market. The fact that a product, its price, quality, packaging, and servicing facilities, are all perfectly acceptable at home, does not make it equally acceptable elsewhere without adaptation to local conditions. An ingrained reluctance to adapt to new circumstances in a new market can become yet another justification for regarding the overseas market as being so unpromising as to justify a withdrawal once conditions improve in the home market. There is, in some cases, a sound case for attempting to sell goods, especially in the consumer field, on the basis that they are different from the norm in the market and so having a special cachet. But all too often the fact that goods offered in a new market are not acceptable arises less from a wish to exploit any cachet of this sort, than from unwillingness to take the trouble to find out what the customer really wants – to be production-orientated rather than marketing-orientated – to use one of the marketing phrases currently in vogue; even less defensibly, to be orientated to conditions prevailing in the wrong market.

The 'Either / Or' Fallacy

There is a tendency among some firms to assume an 'either / or' criterion of home versus overseas marketing, based on the assumption that a large profit at home is better than a small profit overseas. So indeed it is. But it is better to take both the large *and* the small profit. A bicycle manufacturer might, for example, find that he can make a £5 profit on a bicycle sold at home, or £2 on a bicycle sold overseas. If he can sell all he can produce in the home market, he is either pursuing the wrong pricing policy or seriously underproducing, and he would be better advised to consider selling as many as he can in the home market and then as many as he can overseas as well. But he must remember that overseas commitments cannot be arbitrarily repudiated whenever the home market looks better. As a long-term policy, and considering that the demand for bicycles could decline rapidly in a single market, he should take out the insurance of another market overseas. Again, if he examines his system of allocating costs and the prospect of lowering unit costs by increased production, he might well find that his initial calculation of the disparity in profits between home and overseas depends on an arbitrary allocation of overhead costs based on home market conditions only. They might not be appropriate if the export market was added. If overhead costs can be written off against home market production, could not the marginal costs only of production for overseas be considered? On this interpretation, a very different profit rating would emerge. It is not intended at this stage to argue which would be the proper method of costing in any particular circumstance. But an assumption that a market with lower profits can be sacrificed, ignores the possibility that both profits can be sought simultaneously and that each market reinforces the other.

HOME AND OVERSEAS MARKETS – A TWO-WAY RELATIONSHIP

It is obvious that a healthy home market is an ideal base from which to launch an export campaign. The benefits of a large, prosperous home market help to explain the technical competence of American production, combining relatively low costs with high wages, and provide much of the basis of the economic argument for British membership of the Common Market, or any other trade bloc which would make for an enlarged 'home' market of 180 millions, i.e. the original 'Six'. Not merely would the absence of tariff barriers give, for example, a German exporter an advantage in selling in other member countries of the Common Market, but the scale of production which became possible in so vast a home market could lower his unit costs to such a point that he would become a much more formidable competitor in Britain and elsewhere in the world outside the Common Market bloc.

But the relation between home and overseas markets is two-way. If a healthy home market is an excellent base for a successful export campaign, then a successful export campaign with the prospects of lower unit costs is the best way to protect the home market from ultimate encroachment. This is a point which has long been apparent to manufacturers in the smaller industrialised countries of Europe whose home markets constituted the bulk of the total markets of the firms concerned. It is the basis of the proposition, which is receiving growing acceptance, that many underdeveloped countries can create modern industries only if they start from the assumption that the home market of the infant industry will be inadequate and that production can be built up only on the basis of exporting from the very outset.

The implications of this two-way working relationship between home and overseas markets can be profound. For it follows that many manufacturers who would claim to have examined rationally the merits of exporting, and to have decided against it, may have done so on the assumption that the choice was simply to export or not to export, and that once the latter decision had been taken the home market was somehow almost unconditionally guaranteed.

Recent developments in the British balance of payments casts doubts on the validity of the assumption that any home market for manufactured goods can be regarded as safe. The most outstanding feature of these balance of payments has been the steady rise in the *import* of semi-manufactured and manufactured goods of the very type which the British manufacturer ought to have most success in *exporting*. The causes of the apparent growing preference for imported goods are complex, and price is not the only factor, but the significance of this development cannot be overestimated. If British manufacturers find difficulty in competing in the home market, then their prospects in the export market are going to be that much the more difficult, and vice versa. The best method of defending the home market from encroachment is by a vigorous campaign to win a share overseas. As a nation with more interest than most in freer world trade, Britain cannot afford in the long run to protect her home markets by tariffs or quotas. Any such attempt is likely to have a long-term effect of reducing her competitiveness in the world.

NATIONAL AND INTERNATIONAL MARKETING

It is important to distinguish between two possible meanings of the term 'International Marketing'. It can be used as a substitute for 'overseas trade', a phase which is more appropriately applied in terms of the national economy than to an individual company. A country *trades* on an international scale, a company *markets*. But the term is also used in comparing marketing problems in different countries. The problems of selling products vary widely from country to country. Factors which have considerable relevance in a highly developed market may be comparatively insignificant in a less developed market. A company which has one marketing policy in one country may find it entirely inappropriate elsewhere, with the consequent need to vary its promotion, pricing and distribution methods. It is an open question whether the differences in the marketing approach from one country to another outweigh the more fundamental features of marketing which are the same everywhere. This is a field of study which likewise can be termed 'international marketing', although it is more appropriate to think of it as 'comparative marketing'.

It will be necessary to review the problems of international marketing at both levels; as overseas trade, and as comparative marketing; the one a general study, the other more specific. The first definition is the more relevant here, and one might usefully begin by considering the extent to which overseas trade presents different problems from those in the domestic market.

A number of problems – possibly 'issues' would be a better word – immediately arise. Some of these issues represent the very rare occurrence when things go wrong, and a catalogue of problems represents the exception very much more than the common rule.

POLITICAL AND COMMERCIAL ISSUES

Tariffs and Quotas

The first obvious issue relates to the existence, in many parts of the world, of tariffs and quotas. Tariffs may be used to raise revenue, particularly in the case of underdeveloped countries: more commonly their purpose is to advance an economic or social interest within a country, or simply to act as bargaining counter. The fact that the motives for the existence of a tariff, in advanced countries, do not generally place the revenue-collecting properties very high, is important. There is a tendency to regard a tariff as but one more cost which must be either assimilated or passed on to the customer. The far-sighted exporter should, however, consider the implications of a particular tariff in more detail than as merely another cost. There are at least two questions which he has to consider. What type of tariff is it, and it is likely to rise or fall?

Tariffs can be defined in a number of ways, but the most relevant consideration for the exporter is whether they are being charged as a proportion of the landed value of the goods or at a flat rate per unit of commodity imported. The first type, the *ad valorem* tariff, suits best the low-price exporter; the second, the specific tariff, favours the high-cost exporter in that its cost as a proportion of the total will be less than on lower-priced goods. In most cases British, Western European and North American exports tend to be relatively highly priced compared with, say, Hong Kong products. In this situation the type of tariff might give some help in assessing a rival nation's prospects in the market. A second consideration is whether the tariff is likely to move upwards or downwards. No one can predict such movements with certainty, but intelligent anticipation is essential.

As well as ascertaining the exact size of the tariff, it is necessary to make a close study of the wording of the tariff legislation. It may be possible to moderate the incidence of the tariff by careful documentation and invoicing, and to reduce the burden of duty by comparatively minor modifications to product specifications.

With quotas, too, the exact operation of the system has to be studied with care. When exactly does the quota for the year begin? Is it a case of first come, first served? Is it calculated on the local value of the goods imported? Is it distributed on a historical basis between countries so that each nation's total quota is known? Is the quota likely to be increased or decreased? Any information which, in particular, might throw light on competitors' prospects, merits study.

Other Restraints on Trade

Apart from tariffs and quotas there are in existence a number of other restraints which, while less readily defined, are nevertheless important in some markets. Indeed, arguably, they are increasing in importance precisely because the effect of the tariff reductions achieved under the aegis of the General Agreements on Tariffs and Trade (GATT) has been to reduce the importance of these most traditional and obvious restraints on trade.

Possibly the most obvious of these occurs where the buyer is a national or other public organisation, which may, as a matter of policy, choose to buy from local rather than foreign sources. Examples of this are policy decisions to buy local computers or data-processing equipment for the public sector, even where more appropriate equipment could be obtained from foreign sources. Other examples occur with a fair degree of regularity where federal or state tenders in the United States often effectively exclude foreign competition because of 'Buy American' legislation or outright discrimination as a result of internal political pressure. Perhaps the most extreme example is to be found at the other end of the political spectrum in Communist countries where virtually all purchasing is state-controlled and the issue of tariffs is irrelevant.

Other types of restraints are to be found in anti-dumping legislation. Virtually every national government reserves for itself the right to prevent low-cost imports threatening local production, and an implied threat to use these can produce 'voluntary' restraints on imports even without these actually being invoked. Another example of restraints can be seen in the operation of the domestic tax system. Thus tax adjustment on the value-added principle may permit repayment of taxes on exports and the corresponding imposition of taxes on imports which are not officially regarded as customs duties: while the general principle of value-added taxation is widely accepted there can be room for argument on interpretation, e.g. when such activities verge on subsidising exports and loading non-tariff taxation on imports.

Most pernicious of all because most difficult to define, anticipate, or challenge is the use of ostensibly non-tariff legislation to discriminate against imports. This is not merely a problem in international trade. In a federal government system with free trade obligatory among the provinces or states (as in the United States) there is a temptation to use, for example, health legislation to limit the import of fruit or foodstuffs which threaten local industry. There are instances where such health or safety regulations or simple bureaucracy can be used as unofficial but effective restraints on imports also.

Foreign Currencies

It would appear to be most convenient for an exporter to receive payment in his national currency, since this would reduce to a minimum the element of difference between home and overseas marketing. When payment is accepted in a foreign currency, certain questions must be faced on the vexed issue of devaluation (or more rarely the upwards revaluation) of that currency. This can substantially change the value of an export sale between consignment and payment. Businessmen in the United Kingdom have been too preoccupied with the prospects and consequences of a sterling devaluation to realise that some other currencies have from time to time been in an even more parlous state. The general principle therefore is to try to get payment designated in the buyer's currency if this is stronger than one's own. It is surprising how many British exporters in the early 1970s, when sterling was sinking lower and lower in the world's foreign exchange markets, continued to invoice in sterling and so let the benefits pass on to the buyers of their products.

Governments' Attitude to Exporters

An exporter can expect far more positive support from his own government than he is ever likely to enjoy in the home market. A vast government effort is extended to help the exporter in the late-twentieth century, on a scale which could not have been envisaged a generation earlier. Where there is room still for more action, improvement in the next few years can be taken for granted. Indeed, one of the psychological barriers to the adequate use of these resources is their very prodigality, in the sense that many a businessman who regards the activities of government agencies as at best neutral and at worst inimical to his efforts to increase profits at home, finds it difficult to accept their changed role overseas; government facilities are often ignored or undervalued in consequence.

Conflict of Laws and Legal Interpretation

Commercial law and practice differ from one country to another. So also does the ease or difficulty of a foreigner obtaining redress. In most developed nations a foreigner is under no obvious disadvantage if a legal dispute arises; but even where the possibility of unfair treatment does not arise, the problems of raising an action in a foreign country can be difficult. No businessman likes going to law if he can possibly avoid it; foreign law courts are a hazard, and foreign litigation is expensive.

One obvious moral is that very stringent precautions have to be taken to establish when a contract is deemed to have been fulfilled. Books on commercial practice rightly spend a good deal of time dealing with, for example, the type of 'delivery clause' applicable in any transaction and with the need for punctilious accuracy in the documentation of exporting. The point is indeed vital, for, among other consequences, the exact wording of a particular export contract will indicate at what point the buyer's responsibilities begin and the seller's end, and in the absence of a physical handing-over of goods this can be important.

Conflicts of this nature may also arise from differences in definition. Obviously it is desirable that, for example, industrial classification of goods should be the same the world over, and attempts are being made through the efforts of United Nations' organisations to achieve a measure of commercial and industrial standardisation. But it can happen, and does, that differences of interpretation and hence perhaps in tariff duties, can arise because one country uses slightly different nomenclature. It is impossible to avoid this problem entirely but, in effect, it rarely arises in the case of the usual commodities featured in international trade. (See the note on the Brussels Nomenclature in the Glossary, p. 161 below.)

Creditworthiness – National and Individual

A source of misunderstanding which can arise in international marketing is the confusion of the creditworthiness of an individual with that of a nation, and vice versa. The British government would welcome an order which brought in dollars or deutschmarks; it would be less enthusiastic about a sale to a country whose currency was in a parlous state. But it does not follow that *any* dollar order is better than *any* order in a shakier currency; obviously one must also consider the creditworthiness of the *customer*, which does not necessarily reflect that of the currency. More than one exporter has sold in uncertain economic conditions to shakily-based economies and, having taken elementary precautions, has made money. He has then lost a considerable sum in a square mile in Manhattan, selling in what is regarded as the world's richest market, because he failed to appreciate that what is true of the whole is not necessarily true of all the parts, and especially of all potential customers.

The same problem exists in reverse. An exporter may be dealing with an old and valued customer and, having absolute faith in his integrity, be superficial in the precautions he takes to obtain payment, only to find that while his faith in his customer is justified, his faith in his customer's government is not. It can be of little satisfaction to know that the customer has paid on the nail only to find that devaluation or currency blocking makes it impossible to get the money out. In international trade, national and individual creditworthiness are two separate hurdles. To clear one only is not sufficient.

These hurdles are, in the main, currency controls. One effect of the Second World War was to establish a degree of expertise and sophistication in techniques of exchange control which are, in times of financial crisis, only too readily operated by governments. One object of blocking may be to compel the exporter to buy goods rather than to take cash, and if the exporter is unable to obtain redress he may be compelled to buy goods he does not want, or to invest the resources in some local project. A variation of this – one which is fortunately to become less widespread – is the system of multiple exchange rates. This starts from the proposition that imports are to be classified according to their degree of usefulness; that the exchange rate for 'luxury item' payments will be unfavourable to the seller compared with the exchange rate for approved imports.

Transport Costs

There is a tendency to assume that transport costs are related directly to distance. In fact two factors complicate the issue: the type of transport, and the amount of handling required. At first sight a manufacturer might consider that exporting involves far higher transport costs than are involved in moving goods around a small country reasonably well-endowed with transport facilities. If, however, the map of the world were redrawn with distances expressed not as miles, but as transport costs, then the shapes arrived at would indeed be odd and unfamiliar. For some purposes London would be nearer New York than parts of Scotland. The reason lies in the different costs of transport: conventional sea transport in general being cheaper than road or rail, as long as speed does not carry a substantial discount. The relative proximity of every part of the United Kingdom to a seaport gives useful lift to the British exporter. Where he may lose money is in the expense incurred in moving goods from one type of transport to another by relatively inefficient methods and with possibly the need for repacking or opening at ports for customs inspections.

One of the more obvious methods of effecting economies is in the improvement of transport facilities. Standard containerisation, which can reduce handling and the need for transhipment to a minimum, is one of the more hopeful developments; the developing of a sealed container system which can be bonded through intermediate customs is another. More promising still are the technological and political developments which suggest scope for reducing the complexities and expense of shipping over long distances.

The risks which have been described are very much the exception and most exporters will never experience any of them in a serious form. The points which must be borne in mind are that these risks exist, however remote they may seem, but that they are in most instances the easiest from which to obtain protection. Insurance is the obvious way of reducing risk to an actuarial basis which can be costed along with production. For most of the risks described, governments provide excellent and cheap cover. More and more, this question of political and credit risk is being covered at a very low rate by exporters, and in a later part of the book the principles on which the government insurance schemes work will be discussed in more detail. Although risks appear more often in international than in internal trade, their impact can be largely neutralised by the variety of protection for the seller which his government is prepared to extend.

SOCIAL ISSUES IN EXPORTING

Most nations of the world are striving towards a materialistic high-consumption way of life, with the United States regarded as the ideal. This situation, brought about largely by a revolution in communications enabling the underprivileged of the world to see the standards, gadgets and appurtenances of the wealthier nations of the West, creates aspirations which, however remote the prospects of achievement, can be readily understood. In a sense the world is being urbanised and industrialised and, in the process, traditional national differences in taste are being eroded.

But in spite of this drive towards uniformity of aspirations, if not of actual standards. there still exist profound differences in national tastes and characteristics which the exporter can ignore only at his peril.

One may begin by dismissing from this analysis most industrial goods (and in the process, most British exports) which are not particularly social or cultural in origin. It is with consumer goods that one notices the social nuances of behaviour.

Different nations have different valuation even for the most everyday commodities. How much will an individual spend on food, compared with, for example, housing or clothing? It is generally true to say that the proportion of income spent on food, housing and other necessities, will fall as the standard of living rises. But there are still significant differences in the way that two individuals from different European countries with approximately the same standard of living will spend their disposable income. One may prefer exotic food but fairly spartan living accommodation, the other may reverse the choices. If this is true of Europe, where familiarity has rubbed off many of the national differences, how much more may it apply on the other side of the world? Does planned obsolescence mean less in the British scene than in the American? And how does the Spanish attitude compare with the British in this? Or the Indian?

It can be a risky proposition to assume that because one's product and pricing policy, and in consequence one's advertising policy, is geared to certain status valuations encountered in one market, the same policies are equally valid in another market, which, superficially at least, enjoys the same standard of living.

Commercial Practices and Morality

An even more explosive issue is the variations which can arise in commercial practices and in commercial morality. Some practices, on the extension of credit or on the prevailing interest rates for borrowing, might appear to be highly unusual. This is not to condemn them as unrealistic. After all, there are some countries which for decades have had double-figure inflation. In spite of this they have expanded steadily, but, as one would expect, the realistic interest rates on bank borrowing or any form of credit extension will be quite out of line with the situation in a relatively stable economy where inflation is not so marked.

The issue of commercial morality is a good deal more complex. Some practices are frankly corrupt by any reasonable definition, whether the corruption takes the forms of gifts or bribes to buyers or to government officials. However an exporter reacts to manifest corruption in an overseas market, it is as well for him to know when it is an appreciable factor. Where a social climate exists in which bribery is the norm, the local agent or adviser should have the situation well summed up, and the company can decide on its policy. But it is important that the company does know what is being done in its name and not let the situation develop by default.

The Attitude to Foreigners

No nation can be fully understood without a knowledge of its history, and where that history has involved the exporter's country the effects may still be felt in one form or another. Even where there is a legacy of resistance to the British in a former colony, this may to some extent be counterbalanced by a greater familiarity with British manufacturers. In many cases the leading prospective purchasers may have at some stage been educated in Britain.

In other parts of the world, where the British connection has not been so obviously linked with political or military power, the situation has different possibilities. In Latin America, for example, apart from one or two relatively minor incidents in the nineteenth century and some disputed territorial claims, there are few causes of hostility. The British manufacturer will not face that combination of dislike and respect which is accorded the North American. The French, and particularly the Germans, have been able to exploit opportunities in this market. It is perhaps surprising that the British, whose influence in the past has been greater than either of these other two nations and whose policies have, in general, not worked against national aspirations, have not made more impact in this part of the world.

Clearly the impact of nationalism cannot be ignored. As a

generalisation it can be said that the more newly independent
or the poorer a nation is, the more sensitive it is liable to prove
in matters of this sort; and the more dangerous it is to ruffle
the *amour propre* of customers or officials.

One of the most significant aspects is the question of
language. It is both an advantage and a curse that English is
now the *lingua franca* of science and business. The built-in
advantages of ease of communication are obvious, but the
result in a reluctance to learn foreign languages is notorious.
It is, in practice, difficult to assess the importance of an
adequate command of the foreign language, for it varies from
country to country and commodity to commodity. In an era of
increasing nationalism, a foreign businessman or government
official will be the more impressed by a man who has taken the
trouble to master the language of his potential customer. In
selling technical goods it is most important to give accurate
information on terminology which may not exist in the other
language. The buyer in this case almost certainly will have
received his training in a western industrialised country and
be familiar with English, French, or Spanish (perhaps Russian). Fluency counts far more with consumer goods (a local
agent may be necessary) and for rather less than technical
competency in selling industrialised goods. But the seller who
has both has obviously the edge: if the choice has to be made,
it is technical competency which matters most.

Initial impressions are usually created by correspondence,
and this raises a very considerable problem. Does one cor-
respond in English or in the foreign language? Tactically, it
is advantageous to use the foreign language unless the
potential buyer chooses otherwise and provided that a competent translation can be made. A badly translated letter is
worse than one in English. If it is deemed essential to use English for fear of a misunderstanding on a particular legal point,
one solution is a letter in English with an unsigned translation
attached. It is highly important to ensure that where a foreign
language is being used it is being used competently.

Luxury Goods in Poor Countries

In consumer goods the overall importance of the 'demonstration' effect cannot be ignored. The revolution in communications has created demands for commodities and standards which could not hitherto be envisaged, and an amazing variety of consumer goods can be absorbed by the most unlikely markets.

Since, in general, British consumer goods are higher priced than, for example, their Hong Kong equivalents, the prospects for the sale of the latter are better. Price is still an important matter. Nevertheless opportunities exist and, if the mass markets cannot always be won, there is an opportunity to win some of the prestige markets. In many underdeveloped and technologically backward economies there is a considerable maldistribution of resources between rich and poor. However much this is to be regretted in the name of humanity, the market which this creates for consumer goods, including luxuries, cannot be ignored.

There obviously exists a vastly complex picture in trading with these countries whose economies are still relatively backward and whose political set-up is unstable. The producer of consumer luxury goods who is selling in a politically and economically unstable market of this sort would be unrealistic if he expected the market to last indefinitely; it can disappear overnight.

TECHNOLOGICAL ISSUES

Substantial technological differences exist between one part of the world and another. In part this represents a different distribution of the material resources on which modern technology depends, but more commonly it represents differences in the standards of living, and so on the state of technology. There are two situations where the substantial difference in technological progress between the supplier and the consumer can have important consequences.

The most obvious example is where a developed country exports technological knowhow, and particularly where the exporting country is supplying equipment which is also being produced for its home market. It is facile to think of the 'developing' countries as being starved of capital, forgetting that they are also suffering from shortage of skilled labour. Much of the equipment sent or sold overseas is ruined for the lack of simple technical efficiency. Such equipment is designed for use by the semi-skilled machine operator; but what is available in the importing country are highly skilled traditional craftsmen, and an even larger supply of totally unskilled labour, whose background does not include an awareness of the functions and everyday use of machinery. The innate intelligence of a skilled traditional craftsman might be high, nevertheless he cannot be easily retrained.

The ideal type of equipment for sale in such a market might well be something nearer a nineteenth-century cast-iron, foolproof product which can stand a vast amount of misuse, rather than a highly automated electronic equivalent of twentieth-century design which can be ruined in a moment by a single mistake. A machine tool might be a museum piece at home but a practical proposition in a backward economy. So far as industrial goods are concerned therefore, simple, rugged versions of models used at home are often preferable. But if the choice is between the latest model or no sale, a recurring theme must apply, namely that elementary 'commonsense' assumptions about servicing cannot be taken for granted and servicing may have to be at once more extensive and more elementary than is usual in a technologically more advanced market. The problems here are a good deal more than merely technological, affecting as they often do, both national pride and the individual's dignity.

The second situation arising from a different degree of technical development occurs where conditions in the home market of the exporter are less advanced than his overseas market. Planned obsolescence obviously goes a good deal further in more high-consumption markets than in Britain, and the differences this can make to product planning, servicing, etc., are important. Some British exports – cars, for example – were designed on the assumption that the basic model would be in production for at least a decade. Any assumption of a ten-year life-cycle in the American market could be risky. Elaborate servicing plans which are based on the assumption of the availability of cheap, skilled labour would be irrelevant in a situation where increasingly the Americans tend to replace whole components or even scrap whole machines when they break down rather than incur the expense of employing relatively dear skilled labour to locate the faults and repair them.

Different Measurements

Another major technological problem arises from different standards and measurements. Some of these problems exist for all exporters – the non-standardisation of voltage, the variations of electrical component forms, etc. – but some of them are particularly applicable to the British and American situation through the use of non-metric measures. The situation is improving, particularly in Britain where the move to metric measurement is growing.

Personal Visits

Technological problems are more easily recognised than cultural problems; they can be detected as facts, and rarely misunderstood even on a short visit. It is a cardinal point that anyone who proposes to export industrial equipment should go out himself and take a look at the market. Even the briefest acquaintance with the conditions under which his particular equipment will be used, throws up questions which might otherwise never have occurred to the exporter or to his agent. There is no real substitute for the personal inspection and, though this is a point which is often overlooked, there is also a case for letting the production technician or technologist see some of the problems. A works manager visiting a factory may pick out the sort of detail which can so easily be overlooked but which can cause a good deal of difficulty later on, precisely because it is so elementary a detail as to escape the attention of policy-makers.

SUMMARY

The main consideration for the potential exporter ought to be profitability, or at least minimisation of losses, rather than a woolly sense of patriotism when difficulties are being experienced at home. This profit consideration ought not only to be measured in the marginal increase in earnings but also in the increased long-term security at home as well as in foreign markets, which is achieved by widening the company's marketing base beyond the vagaries of a single national economy.

Many problems of exporting are obvious, namely conventional trade barriers, transport, currency, and credit-rating issues. Precisely because they are obvious and identifiable they can be countered. Less obvious problems, however, may arise. Most subtly these may be nuances where the greatest problem may simply be an unawareness that social and cultural conventions which can be taken for granted in the home market are not universal; that practices and behaviour acceptable in one market are not necessarily acceptable everywhere else. Perhaps most difficult of all to anticipate is that in some new markets, technical standards, competence and expectation may be different from those encountered in existing markets, with the consequent need to rethink servicing requirements.

Chapter 2

Distribution Channels in International Marketing

INTRODUCTION

The theme of this chapter is that Strategy ought to determine Structure, i.e. that the method by which an exporter reaches a market ought to be influenced by how he sees future development in that market. In practice, however, the cart may come before the horse, i.e. the exporter may first choose an export channel – possibly that which involves least effort on his part – and by so doing, determine his prospects in the market. The most subtle danger is not that an inappropriate choice of export channel will mean an obvious failure, but rather that the export effort will apparently be quite successful without ever achieving the full potential of the market, simply because the export channel can create its own appropriate size of market which may be less than the potential.

In some markets external constraints may limit the choice of channels available, e.g. even where a marketing company registered in the foreign market might be most appropriate, it may be legally impracticable. Again, where licensing appears very much a second best to direct exporting, it may be all that is permitted. Nevertheless, given the political constraints sometimes imposed by the government of the exporting or importing country, it is surprising how often exporters may make important decisions most casually, and in so doing either limit future prospects of expansion, or store up problems for the future when they may wish to change their distribution methods.

THE SHORT-TERM APPROACH

The choice of distribution channels in any market, domestic or foreign, is partly a matter of company policy and partly a matter of the nature of the product.

A company may choose to exercise virtually no control over the distribution of the products and be content to sell, in effect, ex-factory or ex-warehouse. Generally it does so because it regards its strength as being on the production side rather than in marketing. One example of this might be a company producing industrial components to order; alternatively perhaps, consumer or industrial products which cannot be readily branded, and which are not likely therefore to generate consumer loyalty to be reinforced by advertising.

A producer of branded goods has rather more room for manoeuvre in that he can attempt to promote consumer loyalty which will give him a measure of independence from any particular distribution chain. A producer of equipment requiring installation or after-sales servicing has little option but to extend his influence along the distribution chain. At the very least he has to ensure that his products are being handled by distributors who are technically competent, and he may choose to control the distribution chain himself.

These factors apply also to overseas markets, with the possible additional qualification that if there are one or two more stages in the distribution chain, there may be an equal number of mark-ups to be added to the cost structure: or looking at the situation from the other side, more opportunities to economise by handling distribution further down the line. The other complication in exporting is the one remarked on earlier, i.e. that it may be necessary to have a short-term method of broaching a new market, which will be replaced by a more appropriate distribution method once the market has been proved.

The short-term approach for goods which do not require servicing may be the use of an export house which either buys directly from the exporter and ships the goods overseas on its own account, or undertakes for a commission to deliver and sell goods overseas. Variants on the export house are the confirming house which acts for the importer rather than the exporter, and the trading house which buys and sells in many markets.

In the long term, however, larger companies may find that direct representation in the market, by means of an agent or distributor, gives a more secure foothold in the market.

THE AGENT

The agent is probably the most common method of securing continuous overseas representation and is the most practical method available to most small or medium-sized companies. The agent resides in the overseas market and is paid a commission on orders obtained from that market. Since he is not a salaried employee his remuneration is determined by his ability to secure orders.

He can and should be able to supply market information on sales opportunities and the activities of rival companies. Ideally, he will be visited regularly by the export manager or other senior personnel: many companies additionally pay the expenses of agents to visit their headquarters for regular conferences to meet key personnel, be updated on new products and, incidentally, meet and exchange ideas with agents from other markets facing the same sort of problems.

There are problems in the use of an agent: in the main these arise from the fact that he is likely to hold franchises from other companies; ideally these are not likely to result in his representing competing products, but the very fact that he does represent other lines may mean that he does not spend as much time as the individual principal would like on his particular products and may be satisfied to go for the relatively easy and 'repeat' accounts rather than seeking new customers; lastly the fact of other product franchises, possibly in related lines, may make it difficult for the exporter to extend his range if new product lines compete with other franchises.

Agency representation more than any other method stands or falls on personalities or personal relationships. The success or failure of a product may turn on the energy and ability of a single man who is not really under the day-to-day control of the exporter. Poor agents may improve: unfortunately it is more probable that good agents may in time deteriorate, either because their success brings in so many other franchises that principals who got good service in the early days get taken for granted; or simply that agents get older, slow down and have no obvious replacement. It is always possible to get a new agent for an established product, but it is sometimes an expensive process if the former agent has to be compensated (and national legislation in the importing countries is far more likely to protect the interests of the agent than the foreign principal).

The most subtle danger of using an agent may be that this method may work satisfactorily at a certain level of business, i.e. that which can be handled as one of his franchises by the agent. It is possible therefore that alternative methods, e.g. several agents with smaller territories or a sales company established locally, would have generated more business. The difficulty is that a healthy export market serviced by one agent can mean either a very good agent indeed, or that the market is potentially large enough to justify more intensive cultivation than it is getting.

THE DISTRIBUTOR

There is a certain confusion of terms in export marketing. Some companies use the term 'representative' to cover not only agents, as previously defined, but also salesmen. Others use 'agent' to include distributors, who are buying on their own account, not selling on commission. A distributor will be given a franchise for a particular market, i.e. he may be the sole importer of the product and be responsible for the subsequent dispersion of the product to wholesaler or retailer.

Distributors are most common when there is an element of continuous servicing, i.e. installation problems and after-sales service. They tend therefore to deal in durable consumer and industrial products where a degree of technical competence is essential. The exporter may have to provide initial training facilities, and possibly even finance a newcomer as a distributor in the early stages if the existing distributors have lucrative franchises from rival companies.

The pros and cons of a distributor system are much the same as these which exist in the domestic market, i.e. finding reliable men, investigating customer complaints, and if necessary, terminating franchises.

One important distinction between the agency and distributor systems may arise on the question of pricing. The exporter determines the price at which goods are to be sold by the agent; the latter can alter these only at the discretion of his principal. The distributor, however, may be able to set his own price, firstly because in many countries fixed-price maintenance by the manufacturer may be illegal, and secondly, in some instances, because a distributor of industrial equipment may be able to prevent the manufacturer learning who the final users are and what they are being charged. This comparative ignorance of market conditions makes it difficult for the exporter to judge the true potential of a market.

Although it is convenient to discuss agents and distributors as alternatives, the distinction can be blurred in practice. Sometimes a main distributor will also supply agents elsewhere or even be an agent for some lines and a distributor for others. No great difficulties need arise from the mixture of methods provided it is recognised that the interest of a distributor may be rather different from those of an agent: one is a customer, the other strictly a representative of the principal – and these are not quite the same.

CHANGING FROM THE AGENCY OR DISTRIBUTOR SYSTEM

A problem which may cause some difficulty is that of moving on from an agency system to more direct control of a market operation overseas, by means, for example, of a sales company abroad. The paradox has already been remarked on that in one sense an agent can be too successful if his efforts to develop the market convince his principal that there is potential for direct selling, setting up a subsidiary company in the market to do so.

In this situation, even where there are no particular legal problems in changing from the agency or distributor system, there may be a danger of loss of goodwill which the company will wish to avoid. Some companies intend to use the erstwhile agent or distributor in the new organisation. This may be acceptable to that individual: sometimes, however, he will dislike the idea of losing his independence (and his franchises from other manufacturers) and so may be less than enthusiastic about such a proposal. A compromise solution may be to let the erstwhile agent take up shares in the subsidiary company thus having him directly involved in the organisation without necessarily having to give up all his other franchises.

OVERSEAS SALES VISITS

The use of a sales force operating regularly overseas but based in the home country is most common as a means of dealing with markets in Western Europe, particularly within the Common Market. For such markets the problem is no longer the time or distance involved, since many of the customers are almost as accessible as those within the United Kingdom: the major obstacle is often the shortage of sales staff with an adequate command of the languages involved. Although English is very largely the commercial language of Western Europe, it is scarcely the best tactic to expect a potential customer to converse in the salesman's language instead of the other way round.

Outside Western Europe, the more usual situation will be for the export manager or another executive to make fairly lengthy visits to overseas markets. Often, however, he will be following up initiatives opened up by an agent on the spot; and, of course, sales teams are used frequently to follow up opportunities created by agents, particularly where industrial rather than consumer goods are involved.

Where individual sales are likely to be small but fairly numerous, the choice for the exporter may be between an agent and his own sales force. If the latter is to be used, there may be a strong case for having the sales representatives based permanently in the market.

THE SALES COMPANY OVERSEAS

Sales representatives are sometimes therefore a preliminary to the creation of a more elaborate structure: for example, a branch office employing a mixture of executives from the home company and other staff recruited locally, or even with all the staff recruited locally. Such a branch office may have to be registered as a local company, and attendant problems of operating an establishment in a new area then arise. Where, however, the scale of business is large or the problems of distribution and servicing require continuous contact with the distributors, then a sales company established in the overseas market may be the best long-term solution in spite of the costs and legal complexities. It represents a considerable investment, and so is a stepping-stone in the company's development. Such a sales company scarcely makes a company truly international but once this step has been taken it is psychologically easier to consider a wholehearted approach to international marketing, if necessary through assembly plants or local production.

What are the advantages of the sales company approach? Basically, it represents a greater degree of control in dealing with distributors in the market, control of advertising, pricing, and distribution policies. In many instances it makes the protection of trademarks, etc., easier, and on occasion also the raising of local finance. From the customer's point of view, too, buying from a company which has a local legal existence is more satisfactory than buying from an entirely foreign-based company. It is a good deal easier to obtain satisfaction in the event of his having a grievance.

Sales companies of this sort, which may involve little more than registration, a nameplate and a small office, are not to be confused with the assembly or local manufacturing overseas company. In the less developed countries of the world the sales company may encounter a measure of suspicion, for it can appear to represent the worst form of foreign exploitation – a reminder of the presence and power of the company with no compensating manufacturing or other skills being fostered within the country. But in the more developed and richer markets, where extensive control over all facets of distribution may be worth while, there is a good deal to be said for such an organisational set-up.

Developments from the Sales Company

There is in the sales company set-up, occasionally, the possibility of conflict of interest with the parent company. A sales company is particularly useful when there is a degree of expertise required in installing equipment in a customer's premises or for giving speedy servicing facilities. Additionally however, where transport considerations, tariff valuations of 'knocked down' as opposed to complete assembled imports, etc., are involved, it may be convenient to extend the role of the company away from a purely selling function. At this stage the area between installation, servicing or assembly facilities on the one hand, and manufacturing on the other, may become blurred. If the parent company is not careful the sales company may usurp some of the former's manufacturing role. As against this disadvantage, however, the existence of a sales company may give some room for alternative marketing and pricing strategies. Thus a decision by the exporter to invoice the product to the sales company either at cost, or with the company's profit margin already included, can have implications on tariff duties, taxation, and even currency movements which are not present when an agent is used. Some of these implications are explored in greater detail in Chapter 9.

Beyond Exporting

How far along the possible distribution channels a company wishes to penetrate depends largely on the degree of control it wishes to exercise, and whether it contemplates a movement into forms of marketing other than purely exporting. The next stages will extend the company's influence a good deal further into the overseas market, and a whole host of new issues open up. Most companies, in fact, will balk at going further. Some of the implications of doing so will be explored in Chapter 9.

DISTRIBUTION CHANNELS IN COMMUNIST MARKETS

The theme of this section is that there are advantages in moving further along the distribution channel towards the ultimate consumer even where this policy is not necessitated by the nature of the product. The main exception to this proposition is to be found in the rather specialised markets of the Communist world.

Although Communist countries comprise about one-third of the world's population they remain a relatively small market, taking in an average year only about 3–4 per cent of British exports. In part this reflects a lack of effort by some British companies, but in the main it arises from the deliberate choice of the Communist authorities and their method of doing business.

Briefly, the main purchasing source in these markets is not the ultimate users or even distributors but the so-called Foreign Trade Organisations buying on their behalf and to their own purchasing programme. The individual foreign trade organisation deals with a particular industry, and importing and exporting products related to that industry under the general direction of the Ministry of Foreign Trade.

The great majority of products which will be bought are industrial rather than consumer products, and are therefore items which would normally be handled by technically qualified agents or distributors; or perhaps even by a subsidiary company established in the market for that purpose. The nature of the Communist economic system precludes most of the orthodox alternatives – agents may be employed only in certain circumstances and their usefulness is circumscribed by the difficulty of their obtaining orders directly from potential customers. The most appropriate trading channels for the newcomer to the Communist market is simply to write to the Trade Delegation or Commercial Attaché of the Embassy in London, supplying brochures and technical specifications: or alternatively to display goods at some of the international trade fairs attended by potential users – the Leipzig International Fair is an example.

The Communist markets are highly specialised and are not normally the most appropriate for an opening bid in exporting. It is difficult to forecast likely demand, particularly if there is any element of strategic or military implications. Specifications on orders are exceedingly rigorous and have to be met punctiliously. Although the reputation of the foreign trade organisations for prompt payment is good, an incautious exporter can be ruined by a disputed payment based on failure to meet specifications exactly. Another complication is the penchant of the foreign trade organisations, hard pressed for foreign currencies and anxious to export as well as to import, to seek and on occasion to include a barter deal as well as straight cash payment.

The exceptional nature of the Communist markets extends to other aspects than distribution channels. The contract and probably credit terms are what matters. Tariffs are not an issue and the Communist authorities prefer dealing in sterling rather than their own currencies, and often prefer to make their own delivery arrangements.

AN ALTERNATIVE TO THE EXPORT CHANNEL – LICENSING

For some markets and products the alternative to exporting or local manufacture by an overseas subsidiary is licensing; in effect, the hiring out of patents, trademarks or general know-how to a local firm against payment of royalties. Licensing is in general a second-best choice in that it is probably less profitable than direct exporting or manufacturing locally. Nevertheless, the practice is growing in importance.

There are several market situations where licensing may be appropriate. Firstly, in a country suffering from a shortage of foreign currency so severe that tariff duties are prohibitively high or import licences are issued only for necessities. Sometimes, in this situation the government which refuses to make foreign exchange available for imports will permit payment of overseas royalties if licensing clearly saves import costs.

The second situation occurs where government policy is to build up local industry and employment. The licensing of foreign technology is an obvious way to industrialise without heavy development costs. Both imports and foreign owned subsidiaries are therefore discouraged. Such a highly nationalist policy is most often to be found in developing countries. However, among developed countries Japan tends, discreetly, to follow the same policies, and much of that country's remarkable post-war success has been based on the ability to secure foreign technology on its own terms, and then improve on that technology.

Next, there are the Communist countries where the acquisition of Western technology is an important factor in current development plans.

Finally, there is the situation where exporting and licensing are used simultaneously. It might at first sight appear unnecessary to license out new technical processes in markets which can be supplied by exports. There is, however, a tactical consideration. If a foreign-controlled process is obviously well in advance of local practices there is every incentive for local manufacturers to 'pirate' the process or find a way to break the protecting patent, if they cannot use it legally. There is no guarantee that such a process can be stopped and it may be more prudent to accept the inevitability of local use and at least secure a royalty by licensing.

Products or processes which may be readily 'licensable' are those with a high degree of technical know-how; those with well-known and prestigious trademarks; and sometimes, too, products of a military or strategic value purchased directly by governments. The latter are often unwilling to depend for supplies on the goodwill of other governments and may insist on local manufacture under licence.

The Licensor Company

Thus far this section has dealt with markets and products: but what are the pros and cons of licensing from the standpoint of a company which chooses to licence out rather than export?

The main advantage is that, at least superficially, there is virtually no extra effort or cost required by the *licensor* company. This is most true when the *licensee* company is itself technically advanced and requires little assistance in absorbing the new techniques, etc. Sometimes however, if the licensee is not technically very advanced – in a developing country, for example – the licensor may find himself earning his royalties by more positive help and training of the other company's personnel. In this situation the ideal of costless non-involvement can prove to be an illusion.

Licensing is sometimes regarded as a way of testing a market before exporting or manufacturing locally. The assumption is that if the licensee company is successful in the new market the licensor will later move in directly, either by refusing to renew the licensing agreement when it expires or even by buying over the licensee company.

There are problems about either method. Firstly, the balance of power changes over the years between licensor and licensee, in favour of the latter. It is not easy to get a well-entrenched licensee to give up the licence – or even to be sure of securing royalties in the event of a dispute. A company which goes in for licensing as a means of avoiding the complexities of exporting and later on finds itself in a legal dispute in a foreign country with its licensee, has scarcely made the best choice. Secondly, any idea of ultimately buying over a licensee firm may not take account of the possibility that the value and therefore the cost of that firm may be substantially increased by the growth which access to the licence made possible.

The major stumbling block about licensing is that it may create a future rival, not only in the market concerned, but elsewhere. Licensing like much else in marketing policy is something which may be done rather casually on an *ad hoc* basis, e.g. if an approach for licensing rights comes out of the blue from an overseas company in an unfamiliar market. The longer-term implications may simply not be considered.

A solution increasingly favoured by some companies is to acquire a share in the licensee from the outset. In this situation the distinction between licensing and a joint-manufacturing venture with a foreign company becomes blurred. Some of the implications of manufacturing overseas are discussed in the final chapter.

SUMMARY

This chapter has examined in outline some of the pros and cons of various methods of exporting. At the one extreme leaving virtually all details of export marketing to be handled by an export trading or confirming house: most commonly by the use of some variant of agent or distributor; and on to the most elaborate method, some form of sales company registered in the foreign market, and perhaps installation and assembly operation within the export market.

What matters in this situation are not merely the short-term considerations – which are what most pros and cons are about – but any longer-term plans of the company. If exporting is seen as a marginal, occasional or transient activity, then the export channels can be determined by the existing strengths and weaknesses of the company and the characteristics of the products. If, however, export markets are regarded as having an increasingly important role in the long-term development of the company, rather more care is needed in choosing even tentative export channels: it is in fact worth remedying weaknesses rather than tailoring channels to them.

Further References

C. MacMillan and S. Paulden, *Export Agents,* 2nd ed. (Gower Press, 1974).

A. Duguid and E. Jaques, *Case Studies in Export Organisation* (H.M.S.O., 1971).

Chapter 3

Finding the Appropriate Market

INTRODUCTION

The most important decision which the potential exporter is likely to make is in choosing his first foreign market. Curiously enough this is a decision which is often made in the most casual way – chance, rather than a systematic search of alternatives being allowed to decide the issue. Provided that a good deal of effort and money is not going to be pre-empted in this rather casual decision, no great harm may be done. If, however, the product or the market chosen is such that the decision is going to be costly, whether or not the market choice turns out to be appropriate, then a more systematic search for markets is only common sense – the stakes are too high for anything else.

Market research is sometimes seen as a panacea: it can however go badly awry, even in the domestic market. In the foreign market the problem is another facet of one encountered before, namely that techniques which may yield answers in the domestic market may be inappropriate somewhere else. This is particularly the case when the political or cultural background is significantly different. Formal market research methods can be used fairly easily in the industrial developed countries of the West. The prospects in the underdeveloped world or in Communist countries are less promising.

THE INFORMAL APPROACH

Often the decision arises from a discussion of the question with a business acquaintance who has experience of a particular market, and on no greater research than a recommendation of this sort the newcomer will decide to try the same market: the 'me too' effect in deciding to export and in choosing a market should not be underestimated. The decision may even arise simply from a holiday abroad when a businessman perceives a dearth of anything resembling his own product or is startled to find the price that products comparable to his own, command in the new market. He may then get addresses of possible distributors from acquaintances, his chamber of commerce, or from an official government source, and go on from there, 'trying the water' so to speak.

This informal way of finding new markets is not confined to exporting – for every new market uncovered by systematic market research there are possibly ten which are developed on a more intuitive basis. In view of the potential expense of formal market research overseas there is something to be said for the approach, provided its limitations are recognised and it is not allowed to impose unforeseen restraints on future developments in the market.

Firstly, it may be a suitable method for non-durable consumer goods or for any other product which does not require after-sales servicing, i.e. a permanent commitment to the market. The dangers of an *ad hoc* incursion into a new market have been touched upon in the first chapter. It is important to be able to get out without substantial loss if the market proves to be inadequate; and this means that no long-term commitments should be entered into by overseas agents or customers – whether these commitments be legal or moral.

The second limitation is that even if the trial run in the market is successful, it does not necessarily provide the best answers, particularly on the distribution side. Initial sales may have been handled by an export house which has undertaken to find a customer; or a delivery method more convenient to the exporter than to the customer, has been used, e.g. perhaps a forwarding agent has undertaken to get the products delivered to a seaport or airfield in the market from where they have to be retrieved by the customer. A long-term relationship in the market may require the services of a local agent or sales staff. The first of these probably, and the second certainly, can only be considered once it has been established that there is a lasting market to be exploited.

Thus far it has been assumed that the initiative has come from the manufacturer. Entry into a foreign market may be even less planned if in fact the initiative comes out of the blue from a potential customer overseas. Advertisements circulating in national papers and magazines may be picked up by prospective buyers, or more likely by prospective agents who may want to represent the product in their own market. The difficulty about such unsolicited approaches from outside may be to ensure that unavoidable losses are not risked; this means checking discreetly on the credit rating of potential clients or the local standing of possible agents or distributors. How this can be done will be outlined in Chapter 6.

In brief, there is a twofold danger in a relatively unplanned approach to exporting. Firstly, that the simpler method of trying out the market may not be the best method of assessing its true potential; and secondly, that short-term solutions, e.g. in the choice of the first person available as an agent, may have long-term implications which are not recognised at the time but which cannot easily be changed later on.

The *ad hoc* approach is less satisfactory when the potential exports are durable consumer or industrial goods which require any back-up service, or any product which has to be substantially designed or adapted to individual markets. In both these circumstances a heavier investment is likely to be incurred and the potential losses become greater. There is a case for a more structured approach, either bringing in a consultant who knows both the market and the product, or carrying out a systematic study of the market – a more formalised market reseach programme.

FORMAL MARKET RESEARCH

The problems of market research in an overseas market are best regarded as extensions of the problems arising in domestic market research. They can readily be illustrated by a consideration of domestic problems – with the proviso that in the overseas situation a sophisticated approach may be that much more difficult, while proving very much more expensive. For this reason it is important to decide whether it is really necessary and what precisely it is being used to establish.

Formal market research, whether desk or field, basically means putting a structure on a problem – and this has probably to be done by the firm. Even where outside help is being hired, the more preliminary work that can conveniently be carried on within the firm, the better the latter will be able to judge the value of the services offered by an outside agency. And the more the use of the outside agency is confined in effect to 'subcontracting' the overseas enquiry, the wider the choice the firms may have in choosing an agency.

THE OVERSEAS MARKET RESEARCH BRIEF

Any number of specimens of ideal overseas market research briefs can be envisaged; often, however, much of the information, while it might have a theoretical validity, in practice is of little use particularly where the export venture is likely to make a relatively small impact on the market.

Under this heading of apparently important, but in practice superfluous, information is a good deal of what might be termed macroeconomic information, e.g. national income, population structure, etc. The relevance of this sort of information in the sales of, for example, machine tools is frankly debatable, though it has relevance on the consumer side. An assessment of the political and financial prospect of a country like India or Brazil is more to the point than worrying about the exact population or national income. Some of the relevant general information is, therefore, qualitative rather than quantitative – and like most qualitative information is, in one sense, guesswork.

'Find out about the market for our product in country A' is so vague a brief as virtually to guarantee that vital aspects are missed. The problem should be structured by some form of check list.

As a first approximation, one might divide the problem into main headings

(a) Size and rate of change in the market
(b) Price and cost structure in the market
(c) Sources of supply, domestic and foreign
(d) The customers
(e) Distribution and sales problems

and then go on to a number of precise subquestions, whose numbers will depend on the product and the market. Once the questions have been posed, an attempt should be made to note against each one the most likely source of the answer. This enables the researcher to estimate how much can be done by desk research and how much by field enquiries.

Desk research which can largely be carried out in this country is very much cheaper than field research on the spot. There are therefore two dangers to be avoided. The first is that of sending someone halfway round the world to obtain information which could equally be got by consulting a directory or making a telephone call in this country. The second is to have someone complete his field trip and only then find out there is some information which should have been collected at the time, but was overlooked on the first visit. This can mean a second, wasteful trip. These might seem such obvious points as to require no emphasis. It is surprising, however, how easily firms can incur unnecessary expenses because they have not thought out what they are doing in market research before they start doing it.

In essence then the amorphous problem has to be reduced to a logical structure to ensure that all the necessary information requirements and their probable sources have been identified. Before one can get all the answers, one must pose all the questions.

FINDING SOURCES OF INFORMATION

The General Desk Research Approach

The researcher should check through the index of any appropriate journals. These include *Trade and Industry* produced by the Department of Trade, together with technical publications directly appropriate to the industry concerned.

As well as seeking hard facts, articles, etc., through the index, it is useful simply to leaf through the magazines for advertisements which might give help. Virtually all the leading commercial banks will have produced free literature relating to particular markets, and a day spent in a commercial or reference library will produce perhaps several dozen relevant articles and addresses. The London exporter has a considerable advantage here, in that not only has he access to a plethora of libraries (including that of the Department of Trade), but he may also use the facilities of foreign embassies or High Commissioner's offices.

The researcher should also check official publications from the Department of Trade, E.E.C., O.E.C.D., the United Nations, etc. In general, cumulative indexes are available which will rapidly yield information on all the official publications produced over a number of years on any particular country or industry. The type of reference thrown up by this method might, for example, be the latest Department of Trade report on a particular region. In much the same way, E.E.C., O.E.C.D. and the U.N. Economic Commissions for particular regions produce regular surveys. The British Overseas Trade Board should be contacted for details of their publications and advisory services.

Most of the information obtained through commercial banks, chamber of commerce publications and other official semi-official and commercial organisations such as shipping or air lines, will be in the form of free brochures, leaflets or even substantial books. Information which has to be paid for is often available on a reference basis from the appropriate libraries, where it is of an occasional nature. Information obtained by subscription includes the publications of the Economist Intelligence Unit. This produces a number of quarterlies and other reports on either specific industries or markets. There are about sixty quarterly reviews of individual countries.

It is relatively easy to get hold of useful literature published by other countries. The British industrialist could use the publications of the U.S. Department of Commerce, or the Chamber of Commerce of the United States. Where markets are dominated by American imports, the American published sources may be more comprehensive than British sources. The publications are intended for American companies, but they are available to non-Americans.

Visits Overseas

However thoroughly research is carried out at home, there remain a residue of questions which can only be answered satisfactorily by an overseas visit by a senior executive. The intention at this stage may be no more than to vet prospective agents, or it may be a good deal more specific. Overseas visits are expensive, both in money and in the time of the individual, and as has been emphasised no one should go or be sent on a vague brief. He must know who he is to see, and what he is to do – and provided with the possibility of a two- or three-day extension to take advantage of the unexpected opportunity to probe further.

WHO SHOULD CARRY OUT MARKET RESEARCH?

Few firms have substantial market research departments; fewer still are likely to have the ability to mount overseas surveys from their own resources, although, as has been suggested, it is well worth trying to carry out the preliminary work.

For the absolute newcomer to exporting, the problem is relatively simple. Either no formal market research at all; or the use of an outside agency. For the company which has already some access to the market, but is thinking of launching a new line or exploring a new segment of the market, the problem may be more complicated because it may be possible to use existing marketing channels and personnel. There are, however, serious limitations.

Agents and distributors can and should send back regular reports and impressions on the market, but these cannot always be used for a systematic and dispassionate analysis of a market because they are made by interested parties who are emotionally and financially involved.

The same problem arises in using one's own sales force for

systematic market research. There is a profound difference between a good salesman and a market researcher. The former is a committed individual, convinced of the merits of the product he sells. His ability to assess objectively the merits of a rival product will vary according both to his personality and technical background. The odds are that a highly qualified man in an industry where technology counts for a good deal will be more dispassionate about the merits of a rival product than someone in a consumer goods industry where the hard sell is vastly more important. Highly trained and technically competent salesmen should be positively committed to the merits of their products. A market researcher, on the other hand, has to be objective on the merits of the product. While it may be possible to transform a salesman in time into a market researcher, or vice versa, it is unrealistic to consider taking a hard-sell salesman off his main job for a month or two to do a dispassionate market research job, and then switch him back. It would be an outstanding man who could make the second adjustment back.

Two examples of the problems which can arise illustrate the difficulty. How does a salesman define a promising market? More often than not, by the number of sales he can make in it. Conceivably, if he is a very good salesman, is lucky, or faces little competition, he will do well in a market which may by any objective assessment be limited. A rival firm may choose to withdraw salesmen from a relatively unpromising or a declining market. The company which persists in the market may find that temporarily its sales expand, and its salesmen will possibly regard this as a market with considerable potential. The reverse is also true. It would take a superhumanly objective salesman (a contradiction in terms) to admit that in a market in which he did badly, it was neither the market nor the product which was at fault.

If a salesman is asked to make a market research study along with his normal duties, he may regard a favourable response to a market research survey question as the opportunity for a sale, and the customer may hesitate to offer any information which could expose him to a future sales pitch. An essential prerequisite of market research is the need to assure the interviewee that any information given by him will be used only in connection with the project; his anonymity will, where necessary, be protected; above all that co-operation will not be abused in a disguised sales effort.

What can reasonably be expected from the sales force are regular reports and impressions of the market, for example, warning of a new product, or a change in price or marketing strategy by a competitor, i.e. the type of information which will come the way of the salesman or agent in the course of normal business, and not as the result of a particular directive to gather information on a specific issue. This kind of information is often available somewhere but is not always used, because the weekly or monthly report on which it is recorded is not complete, or its significance is not appreciated by the people who see the reports and who regard them primarily as a means of controlling the sales force, and not as a prime source of market research. Market research in general, and overseas market research in particular, is not easily handled as a part-time occupation. It requires the closest attention from a well-qualified team and, for a project of any complexity, it may be cheaper in the long run to hire outside help than to improvise.

SELECTING AN OUTSIDE AGENCY

The most important consideration in choosing an agency to research a foreign market is simply experience of that market. This implies three possible choices: firstly, a well-established agency probably American or British with foreign branches; a domestic agency with an associate in the foreign market; or more directly an approach to an agency within the market.

Little need be said about the first choice. The second choice has more imponderables. The exporter may have had experience of the work of the local company and be satisfied with its competence. Sometimes, however, an associate relationship may mean only that two agencies in different countries have a mutual arrangement to share a commission if one agency finds a client for the other. It is desirable to find out what, if anything, the associate status really means, and ensure the local agency feels it has something to lose from a job poorly carried out by its associate. For overseas agencies or agencies which operate internationally the best sources are lists provided either nationally by the appropriate Market Research Society or internationally through the ESOMAR group to which national societies adhere. The British Market Research Society or the Industrial Market Research Association are useful sources. More importantly, government organisations such as the British Overseas Trade Board not only give useful advice on the subject but on occasion may be prepared to meet some of the heavy expense of overseas market research.

REACTIONS TO MARKET RESEARCH ENQUIRIES

A problem of all field research is to get co-operation. It is obviously not in the interests of those being interviewed to give up their valuable time to answer questions. The reluctance to give interviews is increased by the distressing tendency of 'sales pitches' to be disguised as market research enquiries. The situation is most difficult in industrial surveys. Consumer market enquiries may make the interviewee feel vaguely flattered and so co-operative; or if he or she refuses to co-operate the point will be clear. In industrial market research, the wrong person may be interviewed and give opinions which will be recorded as authoritative, even though the person may not in practice make the decisions in real-life situations on which he is commenting.

Additionally in some parts of the world, and not merely the underdeveloped world, businessmen are secretive and highly suspicious of outside enquiries: they may refuse to co-operate, or may give rather unreliable information. Again in this situation an outright refusal is better than dubious information. In Communist countries, field research is liable to be regarded as simple espionage and treated accordingly. Any research therefore has to be done by local agencies, and in the light of the comments made before, is of very limited use.

The above comments refer to personal interviews or telephone enquiries. Postal questionnaires can be used, but with the disadvantages such methods have at home. A low response rate may be expected, and those who do reply may not be an unbiased selection. Even such minor delays as the difficulty of supplying a stamped addressed envelope lessens the response rate. All of these add up to the proposition that though overseas market research of a formal nature is not impossible, it is expensive since it has almost certainly to be administered from within the market by a reputable local agency – if such an organisation exists.

THE NEED FOR CONTINUING RESEARCH

It is only too easy to regard any survey as a 'one-off' job which gives a Yes/No answer on whether to attempt a market. But markets are dynamic – the good prospect today may be less attractive next year and vice versa. Continuing research is important even if this amounts to little more than reading and filing relevant news items on the market. If a market has to be resurveyed, it is easier and cheaper not to have to start again from scratch.

SUMMARY

Market research in a foreign market can be even more expensive than domestic market research, and possibly less reliable. There is a strong case for the potential exporter spending some time on a 'do-it-yourself' operation, at least identifying published source materials and making use of the free or heavily subsidised sources made available by the Department of Trade, Commerce or equivalent. This has two advantages:

(a) it will enable him to screen out some markets inexpensively.

(b) it will enable him better to assess proposals submitted by an outside agency.

For many companies or products the best step is a relatively informal one, namely an exploratory visit to the market by a senior executive. If more quantitative work has to be done it will pay to get an experienced agency to help out, recognising however that in many markets sophisticated MR techniques have limited value.

Suggested Steps

1. Do your own preliminary desk research if possible: remember that much valuable information is probably available free through official sources.
2. Do not visit a market until a reasonable number of useful addresses are known: visit the commercial attaché or his equivalent, but let him know in advance the areas in which you are interested.
3. As with desk research, the most valuable sources of information are likely to be the most obvious, i.e. banks, and prominent businessmen whose names are supplied by the Commercial Attachés, banks, chambers of commerce, commercial contacts, etc.
4. Check if some of the burden of organisation and expense can be met from official sources, e.g. by going on a sponsored visit.

Further References

Hints to Businessmen visiting. . . . Issued by the Department of Trade for every major market.
The International Directory of Market Research Organisations (The Market Research Society, 1973).

Chapter 4

Product Policy, Costs and Pricing in Overseas Markets

INTRODUCTION

It is probably in product policy, and the related aspects of costs and pricing, that exporting realities diverge most obviously from marketing theory. Even, however, in domestic marketing few companies practice very systematic product search procedures, but instead introduce new products on a fairly intuitive basis and phase out a product only when it is palpably failing and something is available as a replacement. Pricing in most instances is cost-plus or some form of finding a conventionally acceptable level in the market. Few companies are prepared to experiment with prices, both because they do not have available the convenient price schedules taken for granted by economic theorists and because they are wary of reactions from competitors if they do vary prices.

If theory tends to be overshadowed by marketing realities in the domestic markets, the situation is even more pronounced in export markets, and this is for two reasons. Firstly, any one foreign market is likely to be much less important than a large home market: however frustrating it may be for the export manager, domestic considerations take first priority and any attempt to apply systematically theoretical marketing concepts, relates therefore to the domestic market. Secondly, if the company is inhibited by uncertainties and lack of knowledge in the home market, it may be even more constrained in the foreign market where its sense of uncertainty may be even greater. The only exception to this may be a brand-new (and expendable) market where there are no preconceptions and little to lose. Here an exporter may upset the prevailing conventions by a bold new pricing policy.

If this catalogue of uncertainty sounds excessively discouraging there is perhaps more room for manoeuvre on costs and price than is sometimes anticipated. Basically this is because with the practical separation of markets there may be more room for marginal costing, and therefore different price levels, than would be possible in a single domestic market.

PRODUCT POLICY

There is likely to be a substantial gap between the marketing ideal and practice in respect of product policy as it applies to exporting.

Product policy might be defined as ensuring that a company is producing goods which are adapted to well-defined market segments; that new or modified versions of the product become available at the appropriate time; or that obsolescent versions are phased out before unsold stocks begin to pile up. Product policy can be linked up with the concept of the product life-cycle, i.e. that many products go through identifiable and measurable stages, conventionally described as introduction, rapid growth, maturity and decline. The appropriate market segment for a company to serve, together with pricing, promotion and indeed with the whole marketing mix, may vary according to which stage of the product life-cycle applies at a particular time.

The concept, even where appropriate, is only a crude analogy. But if a company is trying systematically to apply a product policy and finds the life-cycle concept a useful tool in the process, there are still some difficulties in applying it to the export field.

Exports, particularly for the company just beginning to seek overseas markets, are likely to be a marginal activity compared with the domestic market. Even for the established exporter each individual export market may be relatively marginal compared with the main domestic market. Thus, where there are practical production difficulties in making adaptations, the standard model which emerges is designed for the home market. The export manager may not only have difficulties in securing appropriate modifications; he may find that he has a product which from his point of view is being introduced too early or being replaced too late for individual export markets.

Where the nature of the product does allow for a degree of adaptation, two lines of approach on product policy are possible.

The first is to design a version of the product for each market, even if this means so many adaptations as virtually to mean a new product every time. There may then be a trade-off between the extra product development costs incurred and promotional costs saved. In theory at least, if the product is perfectly appropriate to the market, promotional expenses could be cut. The alternative policy is simply to take the domestic version of the product, or a standard export version for all markets and try to adapt the individual market to it. This will involve substantially more promotional costs, or the acceptance of a very small market segment.

In a real-life situation neither product policy will be followed to its logical conclusion, and other aspects of the marketing mix, such as packaging, may be used to affect a compromise. It is useful however to consider the two extremes 'in vacuo', so to speak, and then to evolve a compromise. The exercise at least illustrates the practical difficulties of applying the ideal of market orientation simultaneously in all markets and to all market segments.

Packaging variation is one method of partially avoiding the dilemma on product policies, and this approach is practical at least in the consumer-product area. This aspect of packaging is essentially the promotional one. The protection function and other aspects of packaging, however, are at least as important in exporting.

Different climatic and handling conditions may mean that packaging which is adequate in one market can prove to be exceedingly inadequate elsewhere. Less often appreciated by newcomers to exporting is that different chains of distribution in different economies may affect the rate of turnover. At home this may be a matter of days or months at the most, while the rate overseas may be increased by a factor of ten. Packaging which is satisfactory for a shelf-life of a few months can lose its protective function, as well as its visual attraction, after four or five years in storage. Instructions on the package to the effect that a product must be used within a certain period is not always taken seriously by customers overseas.

THE COMPLICATIONS OF A MULTIPLE-PRODUCT RANGE

An illustration of the problem of reconciling the ideal product marketing policy with the realities in a multiproduct firm may be found in complications involving distribution channels for new products. Some aspects of distribution policy have already been outlined in Chapter 2. Product policy, as well as marketing strategy, will play its role in determining these channels. In many instances, however, the ideal distribution policy has to take account of an existing trade channel for another part of the product line: possibly too the existence of this trade channel may cause legal complications in that the agent or representative concerned may have the rights of a first refusal of a new product.

The existence of a trade channel for other products will change the economies of distribution in the sense that an existing organisation may be cheaper than the creation of a new and theoretically more efficient method. This is merely one more illustration of the fact that what is ideal may have to be modified or abandoned in favour of what is practical in the light of existing factors. While the agent may be prepared to pay lip-service to the ideals of market segmentation, market orientation, etc., for many an exporter, and particularly for the new or marginal exporter, the real-life choice on product policy is not nearly as clear cut as he would wish in a perfect world.

ALLOCATING COSTS

Several characteristics of costs are particularly relevant to the exporter. The first of these is that in British industry generally, and not least in exporting industries, the extensive use of capital equipment attracts a heavy proportion of overhead and fixed costs. While it is essential in the long run to cover these overhead costs, it is possible in the short run at least to distinguish these fixed costs from any variable costs which may arise if a decision is taken to increase production for exporting, without making any substantial addition to overheads.

A second point is that overhead costs allocated to a particular year's production will depend on the policy employed in 'writing-off' equipment over the years, and this will in part depend on the particular taxation allowance system employed. Unfortunately, so far as the British manufacturer is concerned, this may also vary substantially over the years. Conversely, costs will be affected by a subsidy system. The overhead costs attributable to a particular product may vary, according to whether the factory in which it was made attracted capital grants, etc. In addition, any system of 'drawback' or a similar tax rebate on exports may complicate the calculation.

The typical industrial firm is a multiproduct one, and any allocation of costs between the various items produced and sold must be fairly arbitrary. If there is a certain degree of arbitrariness on the allocation of costs, as between the various product lines, there can also be a degree of arbitrariness in the allocation of costs between home sales and export sales, or even as between different export markets. In assessing the allocation of costs it is important to identify factors which are clearly attributable in the export market.

One of these is the existence of tariffs and taxes of all sorts. The extent to which the exporter will be prepared to absorb them will depend on the profit margin available, and the competition. It is unlikely that he will be prepared or able to absorb all of the cost; some of it must be passed on to the customer. Such costs change the lower limit of possible prices. The manufacturer will need to know whether this type of cost is also being borne by competitors, or whether, because of local production or discriminatory tariffs, it will bear less heavily on them. Other forms of revenue-raising, such as excise duties, are not so ostensibly directed against the foreign exporter, but their effects on the cost structure are important.

An important source of additional cost already noted in connection with the distribution issue is that exporting implies more complex distribution channels than home sales. In part, this may mean additional transport and handling costs, but more important are likely to be the mark-ups or discounts involved.

Another of the more obvious factors is the element of risk, physical or commercial, which may in part be converted into a cost by forms of insurance, but which is never entirely eliminated and which is higher in the overseas market than at home.

Next, the combination of cost factors which might be classified as time and interest rates. Payment for goods will almost certainly take longer in the export market than at home, and interest rates will be no less for exports than for home sales. Financing these sales is therefore costlier.

To the factors which may increase costs in the export market, one must add another – the unexpected. Costs often arise out of the blue, and if the cost structure does not take account of this possibility, the ultimate profit margin may be a good deal less than planned.

A manufacturer has to accept that, in the early stages of production at least, his costs, including those incurred long before any goods appear on the market, will far exceed this possible revenue and it will take some time before he shows a profit. A breakeven or a more sophisticated analysis may describe the behaviour of costs in terms of product life-cycle. As has been remarked, this cycle, even if it can be determined in the home market, need not be repeated in the same form overseas. Because of increased competition, increased uncertainty, and an understandable desire to reach a breakeven point as soon as possible, the pattern of costs incurred in an overseas operation may approximate only vaguely with parallel patterns in the home market. Any conclusions based on costs at home must be treated with extreme caution.

A company contemplating exporting ought already to have worked out its own policy of costs allocation for the home market, and this must be adapted: indeed, if a firm does not have a consistent policy then an obvious first step is to correct this omission for the cost structure as a whole, before becoming involved in costing for exports.

There are two extreme methods which can be adopted to introduce a consistent policy in export costing.

The first is simply to identify costs and allocate them on a *pro rata* basis between home and export sales, with the exports carrying their full share of overheads as well as any additional costs arising from shipment overseas. In this event, almost certainly the cost of exports will exceed those of home sales. In a 'one-off' production situation the logic of this approach is particularly strong. It is in practice the more realistic approach as a long-term policy, and especially where exports form a substantial proportion of total production.

The other extreme is by some form of marginal costing. If one assumes that the home market (or some well-protected overseas market) represents the bread and butter accounts on which all overhead costs can be allocated, then the only costs which matter in a new export market are the marginal-extra variables – raw material costs, labour, etc., which can be specifically allocated to the exports.

The concept of marginal costing is more complicated than this if the exports represent more than a small fraction of home production. In that case the effects might be observed, not merely in terms of the use of extra materials or spare capacity, but on the whole scale of production. A substantial overseas market might allow a whole series of new production methods and long uninterrupted runs which could significantly lower average unit cost.

Marginal costing is sometimes difficult to apply in a sophisticated and accurate manner. To be useful, a marginal cost analysis must be able to assess accurately the total extra variable costs on the assumption that the fixed costs have already been covered by home production (or if not covered, are at least irrecoverable), regardless of whether or not the decision to enter the export field is taken on the basis of marginal costing.

In what circumstances might marginal costing be appropriate? The conditions should have by now identified themselves.

(*a*) As an emergency measure to cope with falling orders at home, or to support transitionally a change in production methods. The complications which can arise increase with time, and some of these complications may be tolerable only for the short period. If export marketing is only a marginal activity and the market is relatively unpromising, then this costing method may represent the only possible method of matching a relatively low price.

(b) In a situation where there exists a heavily protected market (almost certainly the home market) which can be saved indefinitely from encroachment and therefore can be loaded with all the overhead costs. The difficulty about such a policy is that the costs, which have not been allocated overseas, have to show up somewhere in a market with a higher price. This high-priced home market is not only potentially vulnerable to the import of goods but also to the activity of any competing firm which either does not export, or allocates its costs *pro rata* between home and overseas sales.

By and large one would expect production for export of the 'one-off' nature to be justified only if it could be shown that the costs include the share of overheads appropriate to the value of the order; here marginal costing would be the exception rather than the rule.

PRICING AND PROFITABILITY IN THE OVERSEAS MARKET

Until the early 1970s it was probably safe to say that exporting in most instances was less profitable than selling the same products in the domestic market. This is, however, no longer necessarily the case for two reasons. Firstly, the tendency of successive governments in pursuit of an incomes policy has been to make it difficult for a company to raise its prices in the home market, even when costs are going up. But no government attempts to prevent a company raising its export prices if the market will absorb these – indeed governments will rather encourage any move to increase export earnings. The second factor is the partial collapse of the fixed exchange rate system which dominated the first quarter of a century after World War II. America floated the dollar for a period in 1971, and Britain did the same with sterling the following year. Floating exchange rates are now common and it is possible for the exchange rate value of a currency to fluctuate by 10 per cent or more in the period when normal commercial credit on most exports prevails – between delivery of goods and payment. While this poses problems for the exporter in fixing a price, the situation has advantages when his own currency is depreciating as did sterling in the early 1970s. If he quotes prices in his own currency his products become relatively cheap to foreign buyers and his order book fills up rapidly; if he quotes in another currency he may make windfall profits when he converts his foreign earnings. The reverse is also possible if sterling became a very desirable currency – but this was a highly theoretical concept in the early 1970s.

Both price controls and floating exchange rates are supposed to be temporary expedients – although the temporary expedient often has the habit of becoming a permanent fact. As long as these two phenomena exist, easy assumptions about the relative profitability of domestic or export marketing will not stand rigorous scrutiny.

ALTERNATIVE PRICING STRATEGIES

A pricing strategy for the overseas markets presents as many complexities as cost allocation. The problem of operating in an area of uncertainty poses some difficulty and many businessmen seek a solution, not necessarily at a point which they can be sure maximises profit, but one which can be justified on some form of logic. At one extreme is some variety of 'cost-plus' approach, i.e. a summation of all the costs involved in production, plus a 'reasonable' profit margin; at the other, acceptance of a price already prevailing in the market, and possibly of price leadership. Both of these approaches have serious deficiencies.

Cost-Plus Pricing

If a manufacturer uses the cost-plus method on the home market, he is not likely to modify it for export price setting and he is presumably aware of its limitations so far as its neglect of demand and competition is concerned. While cost-plus can operate in a satisfactory manner at home, in many instances (the 'one-off' tendering job, for example) its success depends to a large extent on the proposition that competitors in the home market face largely the same technical and cost problems, and that in a sense it is not too dangerous to pay little attention to competition since the competitors' problems and advantages are not all that different from one's own. A cost-plus approach in an overseas market, where the competition is coming from a foreign firm of a different size using a greater or less amount of capital equipment in relation to its staff and paying substantially different wage and other charges, may be more risky. And a traditional criticism of cost-plus, namely the possibility of an arbitrary allocation of overhead costs in a multi-production situation, is even more relevant when the domestic costing policy differs from that overseas.

Accepting the Prevailing Price

Acceptance of the prevailing price implies firstly that the exporter will not attempt price leadership in the market, even though his domestic strategy is based on such a policy; and secondly that he will probably have to work backwards from a 'base price' in the market place, deducting the various costs and mark-ups along the way, to check whether the price can be reconciled with production costs. The pattern, however, is likely to be rough and ready: if there is anything certain about exporting, it is that unforseen costs will rise, and a certain amount of 'fat' has to be allowed for in the costs. And, of course, even if the costs exceed those acceptable for the domestic market, it may be worth considering marginal costing, i.e. only direct 'on costs' not overheads.

OTHER METHODS OF PRICING

Alternative methods exist which give a more intellectually sound basis than either cost-plus or the acceptance of prevailing prices. They depend, however, on a very detailed knowledge or price elasticities in the market, and the ability to predict the actions of rivals. These are difficult enough in the domestic market, and very difficult in a foreign market, especially for the newcomer to that market.

SUBSIDY BY CREDITS

As the exporter moves increasingly into a buyers' market he is likely to find himself involved in giving longer and longer credit terms than he would wish, and at this stage credit terms become as important as price. The subject of credit will be dealt with in more detail later, but in an inflationary situation long-term credits involve an element of price subsidy, which in the last resort is borne by the exporter's government. This situation arises because long-term credits have to be provided either to the exporter or the buyer by a bank, and the credit terms fixed by the central banks may be as low as 6, 7 or 8 per cent even when the effective rate of inflation is double that. Clearly any long-term interest rate which is below the prevailing interest rate plus the real rate of interest at constant prices, is a subsidy. The banks or commercial institutions which lend money at the official export credit rates do so only on the assumption they will be compensated by the government or the central bank. At one stage in the mid 1970s for example, the export credit rate being offered on British and French exports was about half the prevailing domestic rate of inflation: in the case of Japan it was about one-third. On credit sales of five years or more, the effective subsidy was very large indeed. Whether such cut-throat competitive rates made any sense for the industrial exporting nations is doubtful. But the situations suited both the exporter and the buyer, in that the former got immediate payment or was borrowing on artificially low rates, and the latter was having the real price substantially subsidised.

SUMMARY

Product policy tends to be a luxury in exporting consumer goods originally designed for the home market, or in industrial goods where the major home market determines characteristics. Made-to-order goods present no problem in this respect.

In cost and pricing there are two major factors to be considered. Firstly, the extent to which marginal costing for exports is possible in the markets which will not bear a full cost policy. Such marginal costing, however, is advisable only in small markets or isolated ones where a form of dumping is possible. Secondly, when capital equipment is being sold on long-term credit terms, the price may be subordinate to the credit terms, particularly if the exporter's government is in effect subsidising both buyer and seller.

Chapter 5

Advertising and Promotion Overseas

INTRODUCTION

The problem of measuring the effectiveness of advertising and other promotional methods is well known: nowhere is the problem greater than in foreign markets where legal controls on advertising, tastes and cultural attitudes may be different from those with which the exporter is familiar in his home market. This problem poses a substantial dilemma in some instances, namely whether to standardise advertising and promotional methods in all markets, at the risk of being saddled with an inappropriate promotional message in some; or whether to leave the decision to a representative in the local market, e.g. an agent to choose a method of advertising and promotion, with the exporter having little or no say on the matter. The problems this causes are most acute in the underdeveloped world, particularly where cultural and even religious pitfalls have to be guarded against; and also in the various Communist countries where the attitude to advertising varies from puritan disapproval to virtual acceptance. This chapter also reviews some of the conventional issues and subdivisions in advertising, e.g. as between consumer and industrial products, and considers to what extent these have to be amended in foreign markets.

Advertising overseas presents, once again, basically the same problems as the home market: but whatever policy is adopted domestically, cannot automatically be applied elsewhere.

Expenditure on advertising in the overseas market, even

more than in the domestic market, is difficult to decide rationally. Advertising can be very effective in sales promotion but it remains in many respects an uncertain affair, in spite of the various attempts which have been made to quantify the principles.

One of the perpetually recurring problems is measuring advertising effectiveness. It is possible to measure the extent to which the public remember advertising, but even where it can be proved that an advertisement has made a lasting impression – perhaps has passed into common usage as a catch phrase or become the basis of a series of jokes – this is not always the same as proving that it has been effective in its function of promoting sales. The perpetual debate about the hard sell *v.* the soft sell, and the merits of humour in advertising, show that there is little area of agreement. If one is uncertain about the exact effects of an advertising policy at home, the uncertainty can be greater in an overseas market with significant differences in culture which affect the emotional impact of advertising. The typical methods used to judge advertising effectiveness, e.g. area testing, split-run advertising, etc., are often inappropriate.

The normal method of carrying out extensive advertising at home, in the absence of a large advertising section in the company, is by the use of an agency which will give advice on the campaign, select media, and charge a commission (normally expressed as 15 per cent charged on the media, or rather more than 17 per cent as a proportion of the advertising budget, so far as the manufacturer is concerned), and, in general, administer the campaign. The same principle applies *mutatis mutandis* to advertising in an overseas market.

If the firm is relatively small the budget may be comparatively modest, too modest to justify profound policy decisions. Nevertheless, in the light of a decision to use an agency, the immediate question is whether to work through the home agency or seek an agency in the market. The most satisfactory situation is an agency which itself operates on an international basis (increasingly this is the situation and many agencies, mostly American-based, operate internationally); alternatively, an agency which confines its own activities to the home market may have made arrangements with agencies overseas to exchange commissions. Even if the advertising budget involved is big enough to be of interest to the larger international agencies, there is no need to use the same agency in every market, but if a common advertising campaign is to be used in different markets it is obviously practical to use the common agency services.

In deciding whether or not to use an agency with international standing, it is risky to assume that all branches are equally efficient and sophisticated. In many cases, international agencies have taken over existing local agencies with less highly qualified personnel, and it cannot always be assumed that standards will be uniformly high.

Some firms as a matter of policy eschew using their home agent or an international agency to plan the campaign in an overseas market, but seek instead a small local agency. The argument for this is that local conditions are best met by local agencies who may lack some of the more up-to-date techniques but nevertheless know local circumstances intimately, and for whom, incidentally, the advertising budget represents a more important slice of their income, meriting rather more attention. This policy is a riskier one, but if the manufacturer has a good deal of confidence in his own ideas he may find the local agency on occasion serves his purpose better.

The alternative to the exporter determining advertising strategy and expenditure may be simply to leave promotion to the local representative, i.e. the agent or distributor. The latter may be given an allowance for this purpose. A frequent practice is to split the costs of advertising expenses between principal and the distributor.

It is desirable to discover, before giving the agent or distributor this kind of control, whether he is capable of assessing the best advertising methods and whether he can determine the expenditure of an advertising budget. He may have an excellent selling record, but are his opinions on proper advertising worth much weight? Will he use the appropriation to promote his own image rather than that of the product or the exporter?

Advertising is part of the overall marketing plan and if a company has reason to anticipate a substantial export growth the whole question of devolution of control must be kept to the fore in the early stages, including the control of the advertising budget.

METHODS OF ALLOCATING ADVERTISING EXPENDITURE

There is less information readily available in the overseas market than in the home market on how advertising expenditure is controlled. The level of advertising in the export field is only about a quarter of that which would be appropriate on the home advertising scale. There is no doubt that this could be usefully increased if there were only a method of measuring and justifying its effects.

One of the most common, if not necessarily the most scientific, methods is that of the percentage of sales approach, whereby a fixed proportion of total revenue is used for advertising. At its best this amounts to reinforcing success in an expanding market. Declining sales will automatically bring about declining advertising. This is a reasonable approach if a product is coming to the end of its product lifecycle. But declining sales may result from aggressive promotional methods by a rival increasing his market share, and here the obvious riposte is increased rather than decreased advertising to hold or win back the ground lost. The method is not practical for newcomers to a particular market and a possible alternative on something of the same principle would be to fix advertising revenue as a fixed percentage of forecast sales. Such a method depends on the ability to forecast sales, as well as confidence in the product, for if the anticipated sales do not materialise the whole advertising policy may have to be recast in a hurry.

Another approach, of spending on advertising as much as can be afforded, has the merit of being an aggressive approach to marketing which is an essential element for growth in any field. There is however an element of danger in this hyperconfident approach. In overseas marketing there is even less certainty than in the home market. It might well be that a manufacturer, knowing the conditions in his home market and with first-hand knowledge of his competitors' capabilities, can afford to spend lavishly in anticipation of a production and sales run of several years; a situation which can be much more difficult to assess overseas.

Much the same can be said about building campaigns before the goods become available. Volkswagen, in the 1960s for example, following the success of the 'Beetle' car in the U.S. attempted to use a build-up on the later 1500-cc. model, long before it was launched. While the advertising campaign could scarcely be faulted, the model in practice did not sell all that well. Apart from any other consideration, a long-term advertising campaign may alert rivals, and encourage them to indulge in a pre-emptive or spoiling campaign.

In view of the greater degree of uncertainty which exists in the overseas market and the consequent incentive – one might almost say temptation – to limit expenses, as far as possible, to strictly short-term and rapidly recoverable costs, there is justification for the 'objective and task' approach, i.e. a succession of limited and short-term objectives; to build sales to a certain figure, and vary advertising expense until the object is achieved, when new, and once again essentially short-term, objectives can be set. The 'objective and task' description puts the best construction on this essentially short-term attitude which affords some protection against over-commitment in the light of possible fluctuation in the market.

The fact that a national advertising policy is difficult to develop has led to a follow-my-neighbour policy by manufacturers who base advertising expenditure on that of their competitors. The approach of matching one's competitors is basically defensive advertising policy, obviously better suited to retaining one's share of the market as inexpensively as possible than to expanding it.

There is a general caveat which may apply whichever method of allocation is used in a situation where an identifiable life-cycle can be envisaged for the product. An important consequence of using a life-cycle approach in product policy is that it enables hypotheses to be developed about the type of market segment a company should be aiming for at any particular time in the life-cycle, and this in turn will affect its advertising strategy. The complication which can arise is that if a new product is introduced at different times into different markets, the product may be at a different stage in its life-cycle, and the life-cycle may be of a different duration in each market with the ensuing problems this creates for advertising strategy. Moreover, the fact that a product may be a market leader in one part of the world, and have an entirely different role and market share elsewhere can be an important factor in advertising as in other elements of the marketing mix.

In a period of heavy taxation there is a tendency not to make too exact a scrutiny of methods of economising if it appears that benefits from economies will be largely swallowed up by increased taxation. This policy, if related to advertising, is dangerous enough in the home market; if it is indulged in the overseas market it is likely to raise suspicion in the minds of the host government, as when an international corporation disposes its cost allocation and price structure to minimise its tax liabilities in a particular area. And unnecessary overseas expenditure, at the expense of foreign exchange earnings, will invite unwelcome attention from one's own government.

Whatever the method used to determine advertising expenditure overseas, it is clear that advertising expenditure is a function of product and pricing policies. The decision on the segment of the market to be sought carries the company a long way towards determining its advertising policy and initial budget.

Overseas, even more than in the home market, an advertising campaign is a chancy business. It may be necessary, no matter how well prepared and budgeted an advertising campaign has been, to respond to events. If sales, in spite of all the forward planning, fail to come up to expectations, a rapid reassessment of an advertising campaign will have to be undertaken. There are no general principles yet established to determine the allocation of an advertising budget, only *post hoc* methods in particular instances.

INDUSTRIAL AND CONSUMER ADVERTISING

Before looking at the problems of using the available media it may be profitable to examine the differences between advertising for the industrial buyer and advertising consumer goods.

In industrial advertising, while the problems are complex

enough, the concepts are relatively straightforward. If there is any validity to the old division of advertising into informative and persuasive copy, then the former is the more appropriate here. Advertising in technical journals is the best approach and it is easy to identify the most appropriate journals. Some technical journals have an international sale; developed countries have their own technical journals and where a country's technological development is relatively so limited that it cannot sustain its own technical literature, then the interested readers in the country concerned will probably have been trained in a developed country, or at least be acquainted with the literature on the subject in one or other of the main international languages of science and commerce.

Clumsy translations of promotional literature or technical material have been commented upon earlier. The dangers are possibly less acute than in the consumer-goods field. A technical translation may sound unnatural, stilted or even laughable, but while it may cast unnecessary doubts on the technical qualities of the product, it is not so likely to cause offence or complete incomprehension as might a mistranslated piece of consumer advertising. The dangers of bad translation in the technical field arise largely from the aspersion of technical incompetence being transferred from linguistic incompetence. Ideally, one is operating in a market where the sales force or local agents are as linguistically fluent as they are technically qualified – a counsel of perfection in many instances. But where the ideal combination is not available for purposes of preparing technical advertising copy, then both the technical and linguistic aspects must be covered. If the translation is carried out by a competent, but technically untrained linguist, it is worth while to have the resultant copy checked by a technically qualified national of the country concerned to vet it for technical comprehensibility.

For consumer goods the range of appropriate media is much greater than for industrial products. Virtually all the conventional media may be appropriate at one time or another. In the developed countries it is possible to measure in some degree the effectiveness of advertising in reaching the customers, if not of affecting their decisions. Most types of media can be subjected to some form of audit which will show the type of reader, viewer or listener reached by region or by economic group. In principle what is initially required is no more than a decision on a 'push' campaign designed to influence distributors to stock the goods and thus push their sales, or a 'pull' campaign designed to persuade the consuming public to demand the goods from the retailer, and thus pull them through the distribution system. The policy may depend on the quality of the retailer. Are they experts on the goods they sell? Is their advice valued by their customers? Or are they as ignorant of the merits or demerits of the goods as the customer? In some advanced countries the growth of supermarkets and mass-distribution outlets often means that shop staff can no longer give informed advice on the particular product which an individual consumer needs: in other countries shopkeepers may still be well-informed on the products they sell. An advertising policy appropriate for one of these conditions might be inappropriate for the other. But once the decision on the type of policy, 'push' or 'pull', is decided for a particular country the appropriateness of the respective media becomes a good deal easier to assess.

INTERNATIONAL ADVERTISING MEDIA AND COPY

There is a considerable variety in advertising media which may be used by the potential exporter, just as there are many ways of classifying these media. One might list some of the more obvious of these and discuss them individually, first from the point of view of using them in developed countries, and then in the less developed countries.

The types of media discussed are

> Newspapers
> Journals
> Cinema
> T.V.
> Radio
> Posters
> Throw-away leaflets
> Point-of-sale Advertising
> Direct Mail

In the developed countries the advantages of using the first five types of media have been briefly alluded to. The existence of independent auditing facilities, as well as easily identifiable (because defined) economic and social groupings, makes some form of directed advertising a practical proposition. The social groupings used in British audit surveys and official social surveys have their counterparts in other developed countries, together with accurate enough figures of circulation or exposure to the media, and all this information is readily available to an advertising agency on the spot.

So far as posters and throw-away leaflets are concerned, it is difficult to assess their impact, and here the content of the advertising copy is the most important consideration. One qualification needs to be made on the general subject of copy; developed countries are more likely to have stringent legal limitations on the type of advertising copy which may be employed.

Point-of-sale advertising can be highly effective, especially in the mass consumption markets where a vigorous promotional policy, backed up by this type of display and by packaging of an arresting nature, help to persuade retailers to stock the goods.

Direct mail is a sometimes underestimated medium. It is relatively expensive, but can prove to be relatively effective per unit posted. A particular advantage in the developed countries is the ease with which mailing lists can be acquired. Not only are there directories containing the names of most professionally qualified men and women, but it is in some instances possible to purchase mailing lists which ensure that this form of promotion can be more accurately pinpointed than in any other media. And, though the point might seem elementary, the prospects of a sale from a personally directed letter, as opposed merely to a leaflet, are much greater: in many industrial markets the number of prospective customers is small enough to make the 'personalized' letter entirely practicable.

In the underdeveloped countries, media problems are simpler in that there is generally a smaller range of media available but with less possibility of assessing effectiveness. Problems are more likely to arise on the copy than on the selection of media; on the cultural aspects rather than the legal. It is easier to offend unintentionally by using the wrong phrase, image or even colour, in underdeveloped countries where nationals are more liable to read into a situation an offensive connotation, which even if it had been construed in a developed country, would have been shrugged off as ignorance rather than malice on the part of the promoter. There are, however, likely to be fewer legal limitations, for aesthetic purposes, on the scope and method of advertising, and the media presentation can be a good deal more direct and in a form which might well be banned on aesthetic grounds in more sophisticated markets.

With these general reservations then, what are the problems which are liable to arise with particular media?

In using newspapers and journals, the chief problem is likely to be the obtaining of accurate figures on circulation (from an independent source) and the social grouping of readers. This is not too serious in technical advertising where the relevance of the media is easy to establish, but in the more general newspaper and magazine world this lack of information could prove to be serious. Purchase of newspapers and journals argues literacy, and literacy in an underdeveloped world has a fairly high correlation with disposable income. The really effective media to reach the wealthier 'opinion formers' may be the local editions of international newspapers or journals, if these are available, and if local advertising in them is practical.

The local cinema is a particularly valuable method of advertising. One can be reasonably sure that the copy is not being wasted on geographically irrelevant areas. Even more in the case of ownership of a T.V. set (where there is commercial television), expenditure on the cinema or T.V. argues a certain element of disposable income, and here again the medium tends to provide its own 'filtering out' mechanism to ensure that the audience reached is not irrelevant.

The merits of local radio are well known but not always sufficiently appreciated. The appearance of the cheap transistor is likely to bring about a revolution in communications, and the steady fall in price has gone a long way to ensure that virtually anyone with any disposable income can find himself within earshot of the message. There is one factor, however, which must be allowed for – when radio is being used for advertising with a semi-literate audience: the vital connection between what is spoken about on the radio, and what is seen or read about in posters, newspapers and point-of-sale display. An excellent selling job by radio will be useless if the listener still fails to recognise the commodity when he sees it.

The probems of comprehension of advertising copy apply equally to posters, throw-away leaflets, or point-of-sale promotion. Ideally they can all be built round a well-known and identifiable symbol. If this can be linked up with appropriate packaging, the prospects of overcoming the communications barriers of imperfect literacy, or even imperfect cultural comprehension, are substantially enhanced.

When using direct mail promotional methods it is more difficult to acquire substantial mailing lists of the type which are available in developed economies. However, even though there are fewer 'opinion formers', they may at least be readily identifiable by their substantial contacts with foreign elements or by their professional training.

The main problem then is initially one of more tender susceptibilities, more hidden reefs of the cultural, social or religious *faux pas*. A less complex approach than in developed countries is called for; simpler, if not always louder, comprehension; a good deal less of the 'soft-sell' or humorous approach. The ideal type of advertising, measured by media or copy, might seem a generation or two out of date by modern advertising methods. But, in essence, this is a reflection of the situation of the underdeveloped economy; that it is several generations behind the advanced countries in production and distribution. The whole marketing mix, not merely the promotional aspects, has to take account of that.

TRADE FAIRS AND OVERSEAS EXHIBITIONS

The trade fair is an important source of publicity in those markets where conventional advertising is hard to apply, or where an 'on-the-spot' demonstration of equipment is otherwise impracticable; an obvious example is in a Communist market or in an underdeveloped country where it may be relatively difficult for potential buyers to travel abroad.

There are basically three types of such exhibitions. Firstly, there is the specialist fair, e.g. vehicles, agricultural machinery, etc., or even consumer goods such as toys. These may be held regularly in major industrial or commercial centres. These are not specifically catering for international markets but since they attract buyers from round the world, it can pay an exporter to display his wares even when the fair is held in his own country. Secondly, there are long-established annual trade fairs, some going back for centuries; here though there is a degree of industrial specialisation, they are in effect national or international markets rather than specific industry displays. Thirdly, there are *ad hoc* 'one-off' campaigns, e.g. British weeks, in which one town in a foreign market is saturated with promotional events, advertising, etc., for a short period and any exporter is welcome to participate. The effectiveness of the last type of fair is more questionable than the earlier two, unless the transient impact is quickly reinforced and sustained afterwards by individual companies.

Space in trade fairs may be purchased directly from the organisers but it is often more convenient for the smaller exporter to work through the Department of Trade, a trade association, chamber of commerce or similar organisation, where that body rents space and subsequently sublets. Trade fairs have an additional advantage for the exhibitor; since they are officially sponsored it is comparatively easy to get samples or demonstration equipment into the country without the usual customs duty.

ADVERTISING IN THE COMMUNIST WORLD

It is sometimes assumed by potential exporters that advertising in the Communist countries is a 'non-starter' in view of the political attitude towards this type of expenditure and the very practical difficulty of reaching the ultimate consumer. There is a measure of truth in this attitude, but the situation is by no means all black.

Advertising does exist in Communist countries, by print and

sometimes through the cinema and other media. The probability is that with the growth of relative affluence and the more recent liberalisation in most Communist countries of the political and managerial structure, the position is likely to ease still further. Nevertheless, the role of advertising is relatively limited because of the monopoly (or more correctly, perhaps monopsony) position of the trading corporation.

Consumer advertising may be largely pointless even if the advertisements could be accepted, but industrial advertising on strictly functional lines may have an effect and will be accepted for display in the appropriate technical magazines where their effect may be to interest possible end users in approaching the trading corporations to buy. So far as the average British technical journal is concerned, the editor is unlikely to attempt to dictate the form of an advertisement unless he can forsee legal or other difficulties. The method of presentation in the Communist journal, however, is likely to be both circumscribed and largely factual. One can get some idea of the general format of such advertisements from the somewhat unimaginative advertisements for East European industrial products which appear on occasion in British journals on the same field. Specimens of the appropriate magazines can be seen through the British Overseas Trade Board (B.O.T.B.) and chambers of commerce libraries, etc.

In spite of the rapidly changing patterns of production and exchange in the Communist world, it will be a long time before consumer sovereignty prevails even in the purchase of industrial goods. The most effective advertising methods are likely to remain with the trade fairs and, more cheaply, the brochures containing detailed technical information lodged with foreign trade organisations. If the result of advertising is no more than to ensure that these organisations and the industries behind them are interested in obtaining the brochures, then this is as much as can reasonably be expected. The prospective exporter would be advised to spend more time, care and money on the brochures, than on extensive advertising into the blue.

SUMMARY

There are relatively few problems in industrial advertising in a foreign market which do not occur domestically. Consumer advertising and promotion present more difficulties, especially in relatively underdeveloped countries where it is sometimes difficult to find suitable media and to measure the effectiveness of advertising.

The exporter's problem may be resolved into two decisions:
1 To decide whether to attempt a common (i.e. centralised) advertising policy, or to let policies evolve separately for each market.
2 (a) If the first policy is followed, the major problem may be felicitous translation and in general the avoiding of offence.
(b) If the second policy is chosen, then it will probably be necessary to leave the details to someone at the other end of the distribution channel. This presents control problems, which can be limited if some materials, e.g. pamphlets or point-of-sale material, can be supplied by the exporter, and the other on-the-spot expenses shared by exporter and his agent or distributor.

Further References

Central Office of Information: Worldwide Export Publicity.
F. Jefkins, *Public Relations in World Marketing* (Crosby Lockwood, 1966).
S. Black, *Exhibiting Overseas* (Pitman, 1971).

Part II
The Process of Exporting

The next section is concerned with the actual detail of exporting, namely how and where exporters may get advice and help, the decisions to be made on finance and insurance, and the mechanics of moving exports. Although some mundane detail has to be examined, the distinction between the policy decisions of Part I and the detail discussed in this section may arguably be slightly artificial in that the details still form a part of the marketing mix. A major danger discussed earlier still applies, namely that *ad hoc* decisions on the mechanics of exporting may have policy implications which are not foreseen.

Part II
The Process of Typing

Chapter 6

Aids to Exporters

INTRODUCTION

The main message of this chapter is to reinforce two points made earlier, namely that since exporting is regarded as a very desirable activity from the national point of view, it attracts a good deal of support from government sources. Secondly and paradoxically, this support may be undervalued precisely because it is free or subsidised.

This chapter is written from the point of view of services available to British exporters: substantially the same services and subsidies are available to almost any exporter from his own government. The main difference is of emphasis, particularly in respect of semi-official sources. Thus in continental Europe, chambers of commerce are more important than in Britain or the U.S.A. and have closer connections with government. Trade associations are probably more important in countries other than the U.S.A. because of the suspicions in that country of co-ordinated activities by associations which might run foul of anti-trust legislation. By and large, the same facilities are available in all industrial exporting countries, though the source and emphasis may differ.

Exporting is an activity which attracts official approval – and one of the advantages which flows from this is the number of sources which will afford advice and assistance to the potential exporter. The sources listed below are by no means comprehensive but are those which are readily available to most businessmen in the United Kingdom. Very similar facilities exist in most of the major trading nations.

OFFICIAL SOURCES

The British Overseas Trade Board

The major official source of government aid to the exporter is the British Overseas Trade Board. The Board consists of leading businessmen together with a representative from the Department of Trade, the Export Credit Guarantee Department and the Foreign and Commonwealth Office. The B.O.T.B., however, has no resources of its own; its services are very largely supplied by the three government departments, and, in particular, the Department of Trade. In fact then, if not in theory, the B.O.T.B. and Department of Trade are terms which may virtually be used interchangeably for most purposes. It is convenient to examine these official services at one removed from the B.O.T.B., i.e. at the department level. In the section which follows, however, any reference to the Department of Trade or the Foreign and Commonwealth Office implies that the services described will officially be made available through the B.O.T.B.

The role of the Export Credit Guarantee Department is most conveniently dealt with in Chapter 8 on the finance of exports.

The Department of Trade

It is a human idiosyncrasy that one rarely values anything which can be got free or cheaply. This applies as much to the services provided by the government in the export field as anywhere else. Much is made of the fact that export marketing is more complex than domestic marketing, but little of the fact that in exporting the government is not the neutral or even hostile party that it sometimes appears in the home market; instead it is very favourably disposed towards the exporter. Criticisms can be made of the adequacy or the effectiveness of the government's support of exporting; nevertheless the sheer volume of work done – the results of which are readily available to the enquiring firm – represent a vast and often untapped fund of information and advice. Many firms, which should know better, rarely use the facilities of government services, or underestimate their value.

The role of the Department of Trade (formerly the Board of

Trade) particularly is of considerable consequence. In any assessment of the value of this role it is well to examine the basis on which their information is collected.

The Department maintains its links with the overseas markets by means of Commercial Officers who operate 'posts' from Embassies and Consulates, and it thus has close liaison with the commercial diplomatic side of the Foreign and Commonwealth Office (the F.C.O.). Commercial Officers or Trade Commissioners are doing on the trade side precisely what the diplomatic personnel are doing on their side – keeping an eye on economic conditions, preparing reports, and answering specific enquiries which have originated from firms. In the larger markets the Commercial Officers or Trade Commissioners will also have locally recruited personnel available on a full-time basis whose sole task is to investigate export opportunities on the spot. Their efforts are reinforced by the very large research staff of the Department at home, and the result is a commercial intelligence network whose resources far exceed anything which a private company could muster. It is incidentally the F.C.O.'s contribution to these services which justifies its being represented on the B.O.T.B.

As well as answering specific enquiries on tariffs, currency, and credit problems, etc., the work of the Commercial Officers provides the raw material of the standard publications of the Department, such as the Department of Trade Journal *Trade and Industry* (formerly the *Board of Trade Journal*); the invaluable (and free) *Hints to Businessmen* series, which cover virtually every country in the world. The cost of obtaining such publications is negligible compared with the usefulness of the information available.

Trade and Industry lists many of the export opportunities available for British manufacturers overseas but gives detail only on the larger items. Detailed information on specific overseas opportunities is now supplied through the export intelligence service of the Department. Companies paying an annual subscription submit details of the type of overseas customer in whom they are interested. At the other end, as details of export opportunities flow in from the commercial 'posts' overseas they are fed into a computer which matches the enquiries to the appropriate firms subscribing to the service, and details are printed out in card form to be dispatched to the subscribers. The normal subscription will result in up to 500 such cards being sent annually to the firm. Arrangements can be made for more than the 500 if the firm so wishes. In reverse, the addresses of companies who register for the services are available for print-out as a list of product suppliers for the benefit of interest buyers overseas.

The London-based businessman who has occasion to attempt some desk research of a potential market has the advantage of easy access to the Department's Statistics and Market Intelligence library in the city. Even for those who are not conveniently placed it is a good deal cheaper to write, or send someone to seek information there rather than overseas.

These services are in a sense negative ones, i.e. they operate largely on the basis of existing information which has been gathered in a routine manner. To what extent can the Department of Trade (or more strictly the British Overseas Trade Board) be asked to undertake to answer specific enquiries? Obviously an exporter cannot expect a free market survey for a particular commodity or market, but the Department will make enquiries through consular officials, and suggest potential customers who might be interested. Specific enquiries generally produce specific replies. Many firms find it as convenient and rather faster to address their enquiries directly to the Commercial Officers attached to the Embassies in the country. There is no hard-and-fast rule except possibly that the more routine enquiry should be directed to the Department which may have the information on file, while the more specific enquiry could be directed to the overseas officer. What the Department cannot do is to guarantee sales or guarantee creditworthiness; the contacts it suggests, however, are likely to be reputable members of the local business community.

A recommendation of this sort is, as has been emphasised earlier, no substitute for local knowledge and a local visit. But a significant part of the groundwork in assessing a new market can be done before any real expense is involved – addresses of potential clients, for example, and opinions on potential agents whose probity if not guaranteed is at least well regarded by the local community. Even this relatively basic information about an unknown market is a vast improvement on surveying a totally unknown market from scratch. This sort of preliminary information is a *sine qua non* of further enquiries.

A source of commercial information, which has hitherto been somewhat neglected in Britain, is the military, naval or air attaché in an overseas Embassy. The relevance of this particular individual to the average industrialist might appear to be small, but the point is that the armed forces of the country to which he is attached have needs extending far beyond military hardware. Very often too in underdeveloped countries, military equipment ranks among the most sophisticated technology available and when civilian needs arise, e.g. in electronics, telecommunications or transport, the national source of the military technology may be the only one of which potential buyers have any real knowledge. A number of countries, whose armed forces have been based on British models, are becoming increasingly orientated towards the American, French or Russian (and perhaps Chinese) models. Both the Americans and the Russians, for commercial as well as political reasons, have been much more active than the British in using the office of military attaché to further the interests of their own industries in meeting the needs of many of these countries. Where military equipment is supplied largely as aid or on credit from the respective governments, there are limited prospects of sales. But there are large parts of the world where the British military pattern still persists or where the countries concerned are not anxious to be closely orientated to either of the two superpowers, and the main competitors therefore are the French. Here is a situation where a market might be sought which had potentialities going beyond the more obviously military items. The future of such trade channels are mixed. The government on occasion uses these sources as actively as, for example, the French; left wing British Governments however are liable to bar sales to governments which incur their ideological displeasure. This means that even when a Conservative Government is in power, some foreign governments may hesitate to buy equipment which may be refused servicing by a successor government. Britain thus lags a long way behind in its approach to such sales. This is a role where the Department of Trade, as a liaison between the military and political departments on the one hand, and the business world on the other, should have a good deal to contribute.

The Department (again officially through the B.O.T.B.) also publicises and acts as a clearing house for information on trade fairs, British weeks, etc. The value of such efforts overseas varies enormously – depending largely on whether any initial impact made is followed up rapidly and with sufficient determination by the participating companies. In many instances where communication with potential customers is not good such displays are the best method available. The Department, while not involved in many of these displays directly, is an obvious first source of information on the prospects of participation in such events. In the case of fairs in which the Department takes a direct interest it is possible for a chamber of commerce or a trade association to be granted free space in the fairs, the costs being met by the B.O.T.B. This facility is not normally available for individual firms.

The National Economic Development Office (NEDO)

NEDO's chief importance to the prospective exporter probably lies in its numerous publications. In some instances the Industry Economic Development Committees (i.e. the 'Little Neddies') produce reports on the export prospects in their field; there are E.D.C. reports from the appropriate industries on export prospects in machine tools, electronics, etc. Obviously not all 'Little Neddies' are of equal value, but some of them, for example those listed above, produce exceedingly helpful reports and can give very pertinent advice.

SEMI-OFFICIAL SOURCES

There exists a group of organisations which enjoy a measure of direct government approval and a measure of government aid. One of these is in almost a privileged position in exporting matters. The Confederation of British Industries is in effect an employer's representative, something of an opposite number to the Trade Union Congress. With exporting matters in particular, it enjoys a close relationship with the Department

of Trade and other government organisations, has responsibilities with them, in the promotion of British exports by
exhibitions, trade fairs, etc., and in general offers an extensive
advisory service to its members. While not competitive in
scope with the government services, this service has on
occasion a special value in that it will offer criticisms of
government methods and activities which would be scarcely
practical from more officially sponsored or financed organisations. Not the least important of its services are its extremely
pertinent publications.

Of specific interest to the would-be exporter is the C.B.I.
Overseas Directorate which, as well as being able to offer
advice on specific problems, produces an overseas trade bulle-
tin for members as well as reports on individual markets. It
provides therefore the same kind of information as government publications, but as a non-governmental journal has
more latitude in comment and criticism.

Chambers of Commerce

The use of the local chamber of commerce may be the *sine
qua non* for the prospective exporter, for it is here that he will
find most easily available a fund of information and experience which can be readily tapped. The size and therefore the
scale of operation of the chambers of commerce vary widely
but in general, a member company of even the smallest
chamber can to some extent use the resources of the larger
ones.

There are three types of chambers of commerce; the local
organisation which recruits its members from any firm in the
region; nationally orientated chambers, for example, the
Anglo-Israeli or Russo-British Chamber of Commerce; and
(very important in the present context) British Chambers of
Commerce overseas.

The functions of a local chamber of commerce extend far
beyond exporting, but their role here is of considerable consequence. The larger chambers may have regional sections
which bring together a pool of information on various areas
of the world. The London Chamber, for example, numbers
well over thirty such sections in its grouping, and produces

regular economic bulletins on trading conditions in the areas concerned.

The chambers act as semi-official liaison bodies with government departments and have their standing recognised even by foreign government departments. They may issue Certificates of Origin or Carnets for export samples, which can be accepted for tariff purposes by overseas customs officials. They will in addition give advice on agencies, tariffs and a multiplicity of export detail, and on occasion, with the aid of other organisations, mount overseas marketing missions for their members.

It is generally through chambers of commerce, as well as trade associations, where these are appropriate and of good standing in the export field, that the B.O.T.B. will operate – distributing, on occasion, financial subsidies for overseas travel or some types of marketing research which may now be partially financed from official sources.

Quite apart from the official function (which, in part at least, could equally well be supplied by commercial libraries or Department of Trade offices), one of the most important uses of the chambers is that they are likely to provide access to other exporters who have had occasion to do business in the part of the world which interests the prospective exporter, and who may be able to give personal advice or judgment.

Some businessmen, in considering the possible use of a chamber of commerce, think only of the facilities available in their own chamber, and as some of these chambers are small, their export expertise may be exiguous. It can be said that the bigger the chamber of commerce is, the more useful and efficient it is likely to be in this field. But membership of one chamber generally allows access to advice available in other chambers, and not least to contracts with chambers of commerce overseas. British Chambers of Commerce are established in many of the main commercial centres overseas and these help with on-the-spot advice on market conditions, commercial customs, the selection of agents, etc., for the newcomer. A chamber of commerce enjoys certain advantages, in that individual members may be a good deal less orthodox and cautious in opinions than official government organisations. They are best used, not as a substitute for the Department of

Trade and other organisations, but as a supplement. Using chambers of commerce or any other organisations, official or not, is not, however, an adequate substitute for a personal visit to the prospective market by a senior executive of the company concerned.

Trade Associations

The role of the trade association has tended to be suspect. To the outsider it often seems that they exist to further the interests of members against consumers, whether they be the public or other sections of industry. Many of the thousand-odd associations in the United Kingdom scene are, to all outward appearances, moribund – having lived out the original force which led to their creation, and starved of funds by members. Where others have a more active role, this has sometimes been the purely negative and defensive one of restricting competition. In so far as such associations have any active role in international marketing, it is more likely to be as a pressure group to resist imports than active to encourage members to export.

Yet, though the majority of trade associations seem content to play a negative role in overseas trade, there are a number of shining examples of what can be done to promote export marketing. Some indeed have been engaged in the active promotion of exports since pre-war days, but others have, in more recent times, been stimulated by the interest shown by government sponsored bodies with a certain amount of financial resources at their disposal.

A trade association can aid exporting largely in the creation of an export advisory staff and in the commissioning of surveys, visits, and general promotional activities under an adequately qualified export manager. Some associations also produce advisory pamphlets and other publications outlining the main mechanics of exporting as they are likely to affect their members. In many of its activities a trade association may be able to rely on government financing part of the way at least in, for example, the organisation of overseas visits by members under the Joint Venture scheme operated by the Department of Trade which may meet part of the costs of a British firm participating in an overseas fair.

The extent to which the incipient exporter can make use of his trade association to aid his export efforts obviously depends very much on its vitality and the extent to which it has any positive policies on the subject. But, even when an association is relatively inactive, it may well be that some attempt could profitably be made to revive it with the specific objective of converting its main role into an export promotion agency. For it must be said that in a period when a deliberate attempt is being made to foster competitiveness in British Industry and when restrictive practices are attracting growing disfavour, a trade association which is uncomfortably aware of its popular image as a conspiracy against the interest of the consumer, will have every incentive to present itself to the public as an organisation whose role is very much the positive and public-spirited one of export promoter. A manufacturer who is interested in exporting but who feels that he cannot afford the creation of a body of exporting expertise in his own particular field of production, may find that the prevailing opinion of scepticism and downright suspicion with which many associations are regarded, can actively be turned to advantage in showing the association how it can refurbish a tarnished image and give a *raison d'être* to an organisation which appears to have lost its original function.

The conditions which compel manufacturers in the smaller nations to enter into the international field are highly relevant to the British situation in the 1970s. There is a vacuum which could well be filled by the trade associations, in representing smaller firms. Many of the associations already serve a useful function as a clearing house for information and offer advice on marketing problems. It is doubtful whether a trade association could or should turn itself into an export marketing group, if only because of the numbers involved. If member companies run into three figures then any cohesion would be lost, while if numbers run into only a handful then the prospects are that the member companies are large enough to be able to afford the necessary export specialists. Ideally the trade association could bring together about half a dozen interested parties in a particular region and, having aided in the creation of a particular group, cease to take an active interest.

There are a number of important policy decisions which

would have to be made – organisational, financial, and legal; on whether the firms could be producing rival or complementary products; on the allocation of personnel; on whether the group was seen as a permanent organisation; or merely a temporary alliance to gain experience, etc. All of these, however, lead into realms other than the orthodox trade association interests. But all of the issues are at least worthy of study, either by a member company contemplating entry into exporting, or by a trade association which has doubts on its own present *raison d'être*.

The Institute of Export and PIRA

Advice on aspects of exporting procedure can be sought from such organisations as the Institute of Export and PIRA – The Paper and Board, Printing and Packaging Industries Research Association.

Export Clubs

There are a number of local *ad hoc* clubs existing regionally in which local businessmen offer advice on exporting matters to the beginner in the field.

COMMERCIAL SOURCES

The Non-financial Role of the Commercial Banks

The role of the commercial banks in exporting is to afford a supply of credit to cover manufacture, shipment, and on occasion the period after delivery, in the same way as the commercial banks offer these facilities in home trade and commerce. The other services the banks offer the exporter are largely intended as aids to selling their services on the provision of credit. The fact is, however, that the banks do operate very considerable services not directly connected with the provision of credit.

Very briefly, it can be said that the banks offer much the same service in giving informed opinions and reports on potential markets, credit conditions, the selection of agents, potential customers, etc., which are afforded by several official and semi-official organisations. But they are not merely duplicating these services; they are particularly strong on estimating the financial aspects of a prospective market through their contacts with correspondent banks overseas. In many instances a British commercial bank will be both a customer and a banker for a similar institution overseas, in the sense that it may have an account overseas with that bank, and the overseas bank in turn have an account with the British bank. This close co-operation will enable the British banker to offer useful advice on the creditworthiness of an overseas customer and, if the need arises, on his bank as well. As well as its general market knowledge, the bank is likely to have an excellent idea of the general credit conditions in the market; whether, for example, a request by a prospective customer for 90 days' credit represents normal credit conditions in that market, or a suspicious lack of liquid resources. The advice of one's commercial bank on most aspects of overseas market should be sought. Bankers are by nature cautious and a method of payment which has the approval of one's own commercial bank is as likely to be as safe an overseas transaction as it is possible to envisage. The bank makes its living by lending money; the preliminary services which are offered to allow a bank to make a living by lending are therefore freely available. And in such an expensive matter as researching a market prospect overseas, the more such services can be used in the preliminary stages, the better the prospects of a handsome profit from the transaction.

Shipping and Forwarding Agents

These can be employed to advise on the physical or documentary side of exporting – areas to be discussed in more detail in the next chapter. The agents can arrange suitable packaging, insurance, transport to the docks or airport and thence overseas, and the necessary documentation. Many medium-sized exporters use these facilities in preference to maintaining their own shipping and forwarding departments. Not only may the volume of business be too small to justify other methods but a shipping and forwarding agent may contrive to combine export batches from several customers into one freight load, say in a container, with savings all round. The new exporter would be advised to use these services at least until experience of the problems of export packaging and documentation has been gathered.

SUMMARY

The message for the exporter in this chapter is to make use of what is free. A remarkable range of services are available on this basis, and plenty more is effectively subsidised by governments anxious to encourage exports.

Further References

Export Handbook (published by British Overseas Trade Board, 1 Victoria Street, London SW1H 0ET).

Technical Help to Exporters (published by British Standards Institution, 2 Park Street, London W1A 2BS).

Chapter 7

The Mechanics and Documentation of Exports

INTRODUCTION

This chapter is mainly concerned with the actual mechanics of exporting and as such may easily be overtaken by developments. The speed of technological change in this area is such that much conventional wisdom quickly becomes out of date. This means among other things that much of the detail of documentation can become irrelevant or downright misleading. The chapter therefore attempts to explain the general principles and the alternatives available, while speculating about future developments. Specific details have to be omitted.

It is worth emphasising at the beginning of this chapter a point made at the outset, namely that this book is intended to discuss the issues involved in exporting. It is not therefore a substitute for detailed technical advice particularly on the documentation of exporting – an area which requires considerable care, and where the requirements are liable to change very drastically in the next few years. Fortunately, however, such detailed advice is easily obtained from the sources listed in Chapter 6. What follows here is a broad study of the principles only.

METHODS OF EXPORTING

Methods of physically transporting goods can be listed under five main categories.
     1. By sea.

2. By air.
3. By road (roll-on/roll-off).
4. By rail or road/rail (lift-on/lift-off).
5. Export by mail.

CARGOES BY SEA

Nearly 90 per cent by value of all British exports go by sea. Dynamic changes are however occurring in the shipping industry and in rival forms of transport at such a pace as to make much of what can be written about the conventional practices in exporting rather tentative. Nevertheless, it is important to understand the broad issues in traditional practices before considering what is now supplementing or even replacing these practices.

Fixing Freight Rates

Only a small proportion of export orders are large enough to require the whole cargo space in a conventional ship. Most cargoes are therefore likely to be 'mixed'. The problem of fixing freight rates for such cargoes is to obtain an ideal 'mix' of cargoes. If a shipowner were able to combine into one ship's cargo, two orders, one of which had small bulk but considerable weight and the other of which was both bulky and light, he would have an ideal cargo. On the other hand, two cargoes with similar characteristics would represent a less efficient use of the space and displacement characteristics. Thus, the more warning the shipowner gets in advance of the characteristics of part cargo, and the more he can be guaranteed regular deliveries, the better he can plan an ideal cargo mix.

Ally this characteristic with an attempt to limit price competition, and one has an opening for the shipping conference, and deferred rebate schemes. A shipping or liner conference is an association of shipping lines on regular routes which attempts to fix freight charges; there are about three hundred such conferences throughout the world. The term 'liner', as applied here, refers not to passenger-carrying capacity but to regular trade routes being worked by ships. A deferred rebate scheme is, essentially, a system where a regular exporter will be given a rebate by the line with which he deals, this rebate to be paid in the following year provided he is still shipping cargoes with them.

There are non-conference ships and shipping lines which either do not work regular lines (the so-called 'tramp' is an example) or do not join the conferences. For regular shipments it is probably better to use the conference lines; for the odd cargo the shipping and forwarding agent may be able to find a more competitive bid elsewhere.

The conference system is under increasing pressure both from the U.S. Federal Maritime Commission which dislikes the implication of trade restraints, and from other governments whose political or economic interests favour discrimination in shipping.

Examples of non-commercial factors which are of increasing account are to be found in the growth of state-owned or controlled shipping lines. The very rapid expansion of Russian and East European shipping capacity appears to be dictated as much by political as economic motives. Additionally, the commercial criteria applied appear to rank the earning of 'hard' western currency as highly as making a commercial profit. Much of the same characteristics apply to 'prestige' fleets run by newly independent states. Here 'showing the flag' appears to be an important factor. The situation of uneconomic prestige fleets is paralleled even more extravagantly in the unprofitable state airlines of rather obscure nations. All these factors mean that cargo space may therefore be available at relatively cheap rates to exports, in spite of the efforts of shipping conferences to maintain rates.

Another instance of state intervention may sometimes arise from the feeling of some national governments that they are being exploited by foreign shipowners, or relatively isolated by high cargo rates charged. They may attempt to force down prices on cargoes entering or leaving their ports when these cargoes are being carried by foreign ships.

Such developments work to the detriment of the traditional shipowning nations but not necessarily to the disadvantage of the exporter who, one way or another, is likely to find his freight costs being subsidised.

Containerisation

The most spectacular development in shipping in recent years has been the appearance of standard sized containers for cargo, specialist ships to carry them, and port facilities to handle them. A good deal of expense, and most of the risks of damage to, or pilferage of, exports arises during trans-shipment from one mode of transport to another. Recent developments in containerisation and palletisation ensure that the container can remain intact and unopened as it moves from one form of transport to another. Containers are used not merely for the ocean part of the journey, but on road and rail as well. Containers make 'through-delivery' an attractive alternative to the more traditional delivery clause which only requires the exporter to have the goods loaded on to a named ship.

There are still difficulties associated with the use of containers, particularly on the marine insurance side, since it is difficult to insure as 'below-deck' cargo when container stacking has more parallels with deck cargo. Moreover, the container and its contents appear currently to be regarded as a 'package' for compensation purposes, and the amount of compensation payable for total loss is inadequate. Some difficulties have been experienced too in deciding the exact date of dispatch of containers, i.e. when goods are loaded elsewhere than at the docks, and this complicates conventional insurance and documentation procedures.

These difficulties, however, are likely to be resolved in the near future; containerisation is here to stay and ancillary services such as insurance will have to adjust to that fact.

The Through-transport Concept

This concept simply means that the exporter is willing to undertake a delivery further along the distribution chain than has hitherto been the practice in shipping goods by sea; instead of quoting 'ex-works', f.o.b. (free on board) or c.i.f. (cost, insurance, freight), he can quote landed costs at the other side, or even delivery to the customer's own address.

The development has already been foreshadowed by air-transport practices, where a 'landed price' is fairly standard.

Sea-transport containerisation, too, implies the use of the one container from the seller's warehouse to the buyer's – a system which favours a 'delivered-price' quotation.

The through-transport, or delivered-price concept, with its convenience to the importing buyer, is particularly applicable to Western Europe whether by air, road, or rail delivery, and to North America by air. In so far as the importance of Continental Europe as an export market has grown enormously since the appearance of the European Common Market, the through-transport concept is becoming more and more important for the British exporter. In very many instances, his chief competitor may be a Continental producer who quotes delivered prices to any part of Western Europe as a matter of routine.

CARGOES BY AIR

Over 10 per cent of all British exports by value, and probably about 1 per cent by bulk, now go by air. The proportion is likely to grow for the high-value product. Even the qualification 'high value' is not necessarily very limiting. For medium-value products a short air journey may prove competitive in cost to a sea journey which involves greater packaging costs and loading and unloading charges, with attendant risks and delays; particularly therefore in the case of European deliveries, air freight is often a viable alternative to conventional sea transport.

Other factors also favour air travel. Any type of business which depends for its efficient use on the existence of stores, warehouses and inventories of any sort, has a good deal of working capital tied up. It must balance the need for efficient use of its capital by holding minimum stocks, with the risk of financial loss or simply loss of goodwill from a customer if an urgently needed replacement is not immediately available. Speedy replacement by air reduces the need for stockholding, although air freight charges may seem high. The true cost comparison is not between sea and air transport in isolation but between these relative transport costs plus inventory costs. If a company setting up an international marketing operation finds that it needs expensive stores or buffer stocks distributed over several depots overseas, it may find it profitable to consider the relative costs in this light.

The more inventory control techniques can be computerised, the more practical it becomes to rely on a single depot or warehouse serving an international region – even the whole world; provided, that is, that speedy dispatch and delivery can be guaranteed – and that means air transport.

The other major factor encouraging the use of air transport is seasonality. It is now worth while to transport some high-value crops by air for luxury markets; less dramatically, fashion clothes and accessories are readily brought into a transient market by this method.

The Political and Economic Background – the International Air Transport Association (I.A.T.A.)

A dominant feature in the setting of air freight charges is the existence of I.A.T.A. which has among its other roles that of regulating such charges. I.A.T.A. with representatives of the airlines concerned could be likened to a vast shipping conference covering all the regular routes.

The main effect of I.A.T.A.'s existence, so far as the freight exporter is concerned, is to lessen his prospects of obtaining more competitive bids. There is competition, however, both in the price field and in the ancillary services offered by air lines. It is worth comparing the services, particularly shipping and forwarding agency functions, offered by the airlines. Not all airlines are members of I.A.T.A., and non-I.A.T.A. lines may be able to offer competitive prices. Moreover, it is not always realised that a number of local non-I.A.T.A. airlines are in part owned by the larger I.A.T.A. airlines who may not be entirely unwilling on occasion to see freight handled by their less publicised subsidiaries.

Freight charges are fixed by I.A.T.A. for established freights and routes only. If an exporter believes that he is opening up a new market with a new product he may be in a better bargaining position than dealing with an existing market. Air freight charges are still rather *ad hoc* in their application as they have been developed on aircraft costs and performance which rapidly become out of date. At the time of writing, Western Europe and North America represent the best possibilities for air services; otherwise intermediate landing and refuelling charges can make cost inordinately high. But within a generation most of the world will probably be within the 'one-hop' range, and this, together with systematisation of freight charges based on standard dimension containers and pallets, may produce a revolution in this form of transport. At the moment attempts are being made by I.A.T.A. to standardise container sizes by means of discounts on freight charges.

Samples by Air

Even where sea transport is normal it is worth sending samples by air. The favourable effects of a prompt response will often make the apparent extravagance worth while.

Shipping and Forwarding Facilities

Where a firm already uses a shipping and forwarding agent, the latter can be employed for air deliveries also. Often, however, the airlines provide equivalent facilities over and above the actual air movement of the goods.

Sea/Air Transport

A relatively small-scale but growing trade using both sea and air transport has developed in recent years which attempts to combine the most economical features of both facilities. Problems however can arise on documentation and the necessarily complex operation tends to be offered by a limited number of forwarding agents.

CARGOES BY ROAD (ROLL-ON/ROLL-OFF)

The development of exports to Europe by road has been rapid in the past few years. This has been made possible by the provision of cross-channel road ferries with 'roll-on/roll-off' facilities. Provided the exports can be treated as unit transport loads of suitable dimension for the now standard containers or pallets, it is possible to secure delivery by road from manufacturer to European customer with no intermediate unloading.

Frequently, trailers are delivered to the ferry by the exporter or his carrier and make the sea passage unaccompanied. When they are unloaded they are then taken on to the customer using a locally registered tractor vehicle. The use of this system requires only a standardisation of the linkage and braking system between the trailer and the tractor vehicles at either end of the sea journey, and lessens the problems of insurance and licensing vehicles in foreign countries. An exporter can use his own vehicles and drivers throughout but the complications, especially for a newcomer to exporting, may outweigh the advantages.

Roll-on/roll-off transport is most convenient for Western Europe and the disappearance on internal tariffs within the Common Market, as well as the practice of 'bonding' the goods through intermediate countries, is likely to increase the prospects of using this method of export even to European countries which are not E.E.C. members. The use of T.I.R. (Transport International Routier) carnets means that in many instances it is possible to have a vehicle or container sealed by the British Customs authorities, and this system of sealing reduces customs procedures to a minimum in these countries in Europe which have signed the T.I.R. conventions.

CARGOES BY RAIL OR ROAD/RAIL (LIFT-ON/LIFT-OFF)

There would appear to be no great practical difficulty in linking rail delivery through Europe, especially with the appearance of the freightliner system of rapid delivery throughout Britain. The main problem, however, is that the average British rail wagon cannot be used on the continental systems, any more than the continental rail wagon can be used in the United Kingdom, because of the different technical performance, especially in braking. There is only a limited supply of special wagons which can be interchanged.

It is obviously in the interests of the railway systems to increase the number of wagons which can be used in other countries. Of more immediate importance, the freightliner system depends on the lift-on/lift-off principle, i.e. the container on the wagon can be moved in a matter of seconds from one wagon to another, or on to a suitably designed vehicle trailer. Lift-on/lift-off facilities can work out more cheaply than roll-on/roll-off, again subject to the proviso that the containers and their cargoes are standard.

Fast container trains over relatively long distances with lift-on/lift-off facilities available at either end, are obviously highly competitive with road transport facilities. The advantages increase with the distances involved on a continental European delivery. The further south in Europe the market lies the greater the case for rail service *v.* road.

EXPORT BY MAIL

Small deliveries up to 10 kilos may most conveniently be sent by mail. In general the procedure is exactly the same as private posting of gifts, etc., overseas, namely accompanied by a customs declaration form. Customs charges can be paid in advance through the Post Office.

The main difference from any other overseas mail is in finance. C.O.D. delivery can often be arranged, or alternatively postage to a bank overseas for delivery against payment.

ADMINISTRATIVE DELAYS – THE LIMITING FACTORS

It is of little use speeding up the movement of goods if the advantage is dissipated through documentation delays at the stopping stages. Unfortunately, beyond ensuring that the relevant documents are in impeccable order, there is not too much that the individual exporter can do to help.

Where traditional delivery clauses for sea exports involve direct delivery of documents to the buyer, these are normally sent by air. Where particularly rapid movement by sea, air, roll-on/roll-off, etc., is concerned, it may be necessary to dispatch some of the documents with the consignment, provided the documents are not needed to obtain payment, and this, as will be illustrated later, creates certain legal complexities.

A particular problem is that of customs declarations. There may have to be customs inspection in intermediate countries, particularly where delivery by road and rail is being used. This problem is becoming easier, at least in Western Europe, in the whole Common Market. It is only when the goods pass out of Common Market territory that serious customs problems arise. On occasion, as has been noted, goods can be 'bonded' through to their destination. Conventions permitting such bonding are decreasing the customs delays. The chief source of delay may be when accompanying documents are so inadequate that a customs check has to be carried out. Precise details and descriptions on these documents are vital.

DOCUMENTATION – GENERAL

Documentation in any commercial transaction of consequence is obviously important. Particularly this is the case in exporting where in many instances the buyer does not take delivery of goods directly from the seller, or his agent, but via an intermediary such as the master of a ship or aircraft. Payment may therefore depend as much on accurate specifications in the documents as on the condition of the goods.

The great divide in export documents is between shipping documents which imply delivery has been completed, so far as the seller is concerned, when goods are placed in a satisfactory condition on a named ship; and those which imply that delivery takes place at a later stage, after their arrival in the buyer's country, or even at his address. The former represents the conventional sea documentation involving an f.o.b. or c.i.f. clause; the latter delivery by less traditional means. Other documents are common to both situations.

Documentation therefore will be treated thus:
1. Shipping documents for f.o.b. or c.i.f. clauses.
2. Documents for through forms of delivery.
3. Other documents which may be required in the exporting country.

4. Other documents which may be required in the importing country.

Shipping Documents for f.o.b. or c.i.f. Clauses

Although there are many points at which goods can be handed over, from the one extreme of 'ex-factory' to the other of door-to-door delivery by the seller, the most common situation is that when the seller delivers the goods to a designated ship. The two main delivery clauses which cover this typical export situation are the 'free on board' and the 'cost, insurance, freight' clauses – or more familiarly f.o.b. and c.i.f. The former holds the seller responsible for all charges up to the point where the goods have been loaded on to the ship. Sometimes the term 'over the ship's rail' is used to describe, picturesquely if not entirely accurately, the point at which the seller's responsibilities end. He has delivered the goods to a designated vessel; all other costs including insurance and freight charges fall on the buyer. The second clause, c.i.f., holds the seller responsible for the freight costs and insurance cover so that, in general, the main costs incurred by the buyer start when the ship docks at the end of the voyage.

The f.o.b. clause appears to be the more commonly used by British exporters, especially for small orders. Largely this situation, which is often described as 'normal practice in the trade', is adopted because it places the onus of tackling the sometimes rather complicated freight charge system on the buyer. However, with the increasing appearance of a buyer's market in exporting, there is growing pressure on exporters to quote c.i.f. Certainly British *importers* generally seem to have no difficulty in securing c.i.f. quotations from their suppliers overseas, and it is a little difficult to justify the use of f.o.b. instead of c.i.f. where regular deliveries on a routine basis are being made, particularly on short sea voyages, e.g. to European markets.

An exception to this applies where some overseas buyers, principally in Communist countries, may prefer f.o.b. quotations since they may be required to use their own national shipping lines as a means of conserving foreign exchange.

In the United Kingdom there is also growing official

encouragement to use c.i.f. particularly if a British ship can be used because of the effect on the invisible exports item of the balance of payments.

With a c.i.f. delivery clause there are a minimum of three documents involved – an invoice, a bill of lading, and a marine insurance policy. Generally speaking, the seller can be said to have fulfilled his part of the contract when he hands these documents over, either to the buyer, or to another authorised agent such as a bank.

The invoice is, for all practical purposes, like any invoice which could be used in an internal commercial transaction, giving the name of the buyer, price and quantity of the goods, shipping marks on the packages, etc.

The bill of lading consists of a document signed by the ship's master acknowledging receipt of goods which have been loaded on to the ship in apparently good condition. The goods will be described, again probably in terms of a number of crates, with their marking. The ship's master can only des-cribe in general terms what he has been given; he cannot be expected to classify the goods in detail. Three copies of the bill of lading will normally be issued – the seller, and possibly his bank will wish to retain copies. The production of one of the bills of lading, properly signed by the ship's master, will give the right to collect the goods at the port of destination. The bill of lading gives proof of owner-ship.

Lastly in the essential documents, is a marine insurance policy. Marine insurance is insurance against physical risks of destruction by sinking, fire, etc., and an exporter can readily agree with an insurance broker or underwriter what precisely he wants cover against. Insurance disputes rarely arise from situations where goods are wholly lost but rather where an element of damage has been caused, or even where, although the goods have come to no harm, another part of a cargo has been lost or damaged in circumstances which give the owner of these goods a claim against the owners of other goods being carried in the ship, e.g. because part of the cargo was sacri-ficed to save the remainder; here the owners or insurers of the sacrificed cargo are likely in law to have a claim on the owners of the cargo which was saved. An exporter has to insure not merely against the loss of his own goods but other less foreseeable risks.

These three documents, the invoice, the bill of lading, and the marine insurance policy, are the basic documents; the handing over of which in an acceptable condition by the seller constitutes some form of proof that he has fulfilled his part of the contract. He may dispatch them directly to the buyer by airmail and get payment in return. The danger of this method is that, effectively, the exporter has given up control before he has any guarantee of payment. This method can be used only when there is absolute confidence between buyer and seller. Alternatively, the contract may require that the documents be delivered to a bank which will then either make payment or, if delivery involves a period of credit, will arrange for the credit conditions to be invoked – possibly accepting a bill of exchange, or offering credit facilities previously arranged. Some methods of finance and credits which can be used are discussed in Chapter 8.

What has been described is the minimum procedure under a c.i.f. clause. There are alternatives of which the f.o.b. is the most common. The buyer may make arrangements to use a shipping line of his choice, or perhaps take insurance cover in a form and from a source outside the usual practice. On occasion, even under an f.o.b. or similar clause the seller will still undertake to arrange insurance and/or freight charges and be reimbursed by the buyer separately from the selling price. The marine insurance policy requirements would be correspondingly amended so far as the seller was concerned.

Documentation for Through Forms of Delivery

Containers by Sea. Where containerisation is practicable it is possible to use a through bill of lading, a document covering not merely the sea journey but all stages of delivery.

Air Transport. Air transport has no equivalent of a bill of lading, whose possession signifies a title to ownership of the goods. Air cargoes are likely to arrive at least as quickly as would an airmailed bill of lading, and the consequent delay which would occur in collecting the goods by presentation of the document would nullify most of the advantages of speed. The normal air document is the air consignment note or air waybill, which is a receipt for delivery of the goods given by the airline rather than title to ownership. Copies of the air waybill will be held by interested parties, but the goods themselves will be handed over to the consignee designated on the bill. In most cases the consignee named will be the buyer or his agent.

The consignor retains responsibility for the goods during the flight and is, in general, responsible for the other documentation such as the invoice, and insurance where appropriate. The relatively short time involved and the conditions of transport make many traditional marine risks negligible, and insurance rates are relatively low.

Other Forms of Through Traffic. Since two of the main advantages of roll-on/roll-off, and lift-on/lift-off transport services, especially to Europe, are (a) speed which can match the movement of documents by air, and (b) convenience to the buyer through delivery to his designated address, the documentation required approximates to the pattern of air transport, i.e. railway waybills, receipts, etc., which are similar in function to the air waybills.

NOTE: What follows in the next two sections relates to exporting in general. Within the European Economic Community the procedure is being substantially simplified.

Documents Required in the Exporting Country

This section relates to the requirements of the United Kingdom exporter but the same principles apply in most developed countries.

Customs Forms. Export details have to be reported to H.M. Customs, and the normal procedure is for the requisite customs form to be lodged with the customs authority at the point of export within a few days of dispatch. The details are slightly more complex than this, but instructions on the filling in of these documents can readily be obtained when they are requested from Customs.

Export Licences. A few exports require an export licence – for example, scrap metal, which may be in short supply in the United Kingdom; items which might be regarded as the export of capital; some works of art; and, more relevant, some items of military or strategic importance listed under, for example, a strategic embargo list applying to Communist countries. When doubt arises, the Department of Trade will advise, but they should be consulted well in advance on the additional documentation necessary to satisfy the requirements of the customs authorities.

Port Authority Forms. These are more or less self-explanatory – they notify the authorities of the nature of the cargoes and list such items as the port charges to be paid.

Documents which may be Required by the Importing Country

Customs Forms. The Customs authorities of most countries have their own requirements on documentation which must obviously be met by the potential seller. Requirements vary widely but can readily be checked with the consulates of the countries concerned, or the Department of Trade or chamber of commerce. One of the most common of these requirements may be some form of certificate of origin.

Tariff duties on a particular item may vary according to the origin of the goods and it may be necessary to prove that the goods originated in Britain and were not being transhipped from elsewhere.

Some countries require certification of information by their own representative in the United Kingdom; this service is performed for a fee by local consul, who may supply official forms for the purpose. Such consular invoices have to be in the official language of the importing country and conform to the local customs.

Import Licences. Some countries which operate quota controls or have a foreign exchange shortage require that an import licence should be held for certain types of goods, and this has to be obtained by the importer. An import licence may be necessary before currency for payment is made available. It is essential for the exporter to have an assurance that such a licence has been obtained before he dispatches the goods.

STANDARDISING EXPORT DOCUMENTS

In recent years a good deal has been done to standardise the layout of all the documents concerned so that, once a master document has been prepared, mechanised methods of data processing can produce sets of all the relevant documents virtually simultaneously, saving time, expense, and the possibility of errors in the transfer of information from one document to another. Errors arise as much from the boring routine of transferring information from one piece of paper to another, as from the actual complexity of the information; any system which cuts out retyping cuts down the danger or error. Although standardisation of the documents is by no means universal, documentation for export should become a good deal simpler in the next few years.

The British system, known as aligned documentation, conforms to a single U.N. standard and is broadly similar to the methods adopted by other major trading nations.

PACKAGING FOR EXPORT

Packaging is the responsibility of the exporter but he should be advised by the buyer, of any special requirements and should fulfil these requirements rigorously. The newcomer to exporting can obtain advice on the problems of packaging for exports from a specialist in this field, or a shipping and forwarding agent. For conventional sea freight there are two types of problems: physical requirements and legal (especially Customs) requirements.

Even where standard containers are being used extra care has to be taken in packing. There is a vast difference between the jolting arising from normal road or rail movement, and that from a storm. The use of a container does not exclude the necessity for care in packaging.

Goods going overseas are almost certainly going to be subjected to rougher handling, longer delays, and more trying climatic conditions than on an internal delivery journey. They are also subject to a greater risk of pilferage. This means the use of stronger materials; wooden crates with, where necessary, waterproofed lining of zinc, tin, etc., so constructed that pilferage is difficult and, if attempted, readily detectable. Unfortunately it is not unknown for the opposite extreme to be encountered, i.e. overpacking with consequent increased freight costs. Where the goods are fragile, or are to be handled especially carefully, details will have to be marked or stencilled on not only in English, but in any other appropriate languages, and with symbols to emphasise the instructions. Weights, measurements, etc., are normally in metric form, except in the United States and other English-speaking areas which still use the English system of weights. Even where tons, lb., etc., are used care should be taken that the measures are understood; thus there is an important distinction between the long and short ton: English weights such as cwts or quarters should not be used in these cases.

Customs and legal requirements will, of course, vary from country to country but should be scrupulously observed. Identification marks, serial numbers, etc., are required to identify cargo shown on bills of lading, invoices, etc. The consignee's name and address may have to be shown, unless this would identify desirable pilfering crates, in which case agreed marks may be substituted. The country of origin will almost certainly be required, and the port of destination. Weights, volume, etc., may also be required.

Accurate descriptions on the crates, bales, etc., matching those on the shipping documents are essential, and where any doubt exists advice can be obtained on physical and legal requirements from the appropriate outside organisations, both official and commercial.

A number of specific problems can arise on customs duty. The exact description of goods can affect the customs due, a particularly important factor where a descriptive term as a 'luxury' item might attract a very high tariff; where one crate contains a mixture of dutiable goods there may be a risk of charges being levied at the highest rate; and, not least, the customs duty may vary according to whether the goods are in an assembled or 'knocked-down state. Packaging is often a good deal easier in a 'completely knocked-down' state, and since the cost of assembly is not shown in the customs valuation, this is an advantageous method from the point of view of ease and economy.

The same problems apply to air freight except that packaging can be a good deal less bulky; a light frame or even a plastic cover may suffice. But in most instances of air travel there is likely to be movement by road or rail at one end or the other, and packaging will have to be adequate for this too. Here again the advice of the forwarding agent is invaluable.

POSSIBLE FUTURE DEVELOPMENTS IN CARGO-HANDLING

Developments in the physical handling of exports are occurring at a dramatic rate and much that can be written about cargo-handling and the allied documentation is likely to be out-dated within a decade. Yet it is surprising how little attention is sometimes paid by exporters to these developments and their implications.

In summary, cargo-handling appears to be moving decisively towards the use of standard unit loads, either of containers or of pallets; a movement accelerated by rocketing costs of dock handling by conventional methods. Apart from bulk cargoes, e.g. oil, ores, or grain for which bulk carriers are readily available, freight is increasingly likely to be divided into two types: the containerised or palletised unit load on the one hand, and residual cargo, i.e. bulky components which cannot conveniently be handled in standard containers, on the other.

Unit loads can be processed at inland terminals, so as to spend a minimum waiting and handling time in the very expensive dock areas. The high costs which accrue when cargoes are handled or delayed in the docks combined with a buyer's market situation on exporting, i.e. where the convenience of the importer counts for more and more, increasingly implies the need for very fast 'through-service' handling, beginning at inland cargo terminals and ending with direct through delivery to the purchaser. The container or its equivalent will have to be packed on the manufacturer's own premises, to be unpacked if possible on the purchaser's own premises. Door-to-door, at the very least pier-to-pier, delivery is likely to be the norm, and this opens up the whole concept of an integrated transport and documentation system offered by one organisation – probably the shipping or airline company.

The number of ships and modern ports is likely to fall. Partly this will happen because the capital investment required for the new sea and land handling facilities is likely to be very great. As against this, there is the compensating factor that a smaller number of ships with a mere handful of port installations will be able to handle the requirements of the whole British economy. The location of these facilities is likely to be determined by the growing size of ships – relatively few ports have sufficient depth of water for the very large ships, and already the development of east coast ports is being affected by the relative shallowness of much of the North Sea.

There are, of course, alternatives to meet new developments, for shallow-draught ports or countries where the capital requirements of integrated cargo-handling are just not available. Examples of these developments are the LASH (lighter aboard ship) the BACAT (barges aboard catamaran) ships – large vessels carrying and launching shallow-draught cargo barges. The ship will sail with cargo already stored on the barges – a situation analogous to the whole container concept – and without having to enter port itself would launch or pick up barges almost like an international milk run. This would not only serve the non-container terminal ports, but would enable the residual type of cargo, as well as conventional containers, to be delivered with the actual landing of cargo taking place, if necessary, up river of the main port if this were more convenient.

The next generation of these ships, already on the drawing board, would enable barges to be stacked after the manner of present-day containers; in effect containers which float and even may have their own method of propulsion.

The second development in this general area is the considerable increase in speed of delivery implicit in the situation. Container and other specialist ships are enormously expensive and can be justified only by reason of their very intensive use. Already unloading of a cargo of containers at a container terminal is a matter of hours, rather than weeks by conventional handling methods. There is a physical limitation to the speed with which cargo-handling can be accelerated further, and the margin for improvement has now fallen to a few hours. The most promising area for a further speed up is therefore literally at sea. A few years ago a general cargo ship could be expected to operate most economically at 12–14 knots and would probably be pushed to work up a few more knots. Container ships are now appearing which cruise at more than double that speed, the increased fuel costs being more than compensated for by the more intensive use of the capital involved, by at least doubling the number of voyages in a given time. Indeed, unconventional multi-hull container ships designed to cruise at 60 knots are a technical possibility. One of these could, if successful, probably replace a score of conventional general cargo ships.

What then are the implications of these developments for the late 1970s or early 1980s? It would be a bold man who could prophesy with confidence, but some of the possible developments can be summed up thus.

Integrated cargo-handling by container or unit load pallet may become the norm with a consequent decline in the availability of general cargo ships, which will tend to be confined to residual cargoes only.

Since the whole *raison d'être* of these highly capitalised developments is speed, the need to revise and speed up documentation procedures becomes urgent. Increasingly it may become impractical to use a conventional bill of lading, trusting that its arrival at the other end will take place before the physical delivery of the cargo it represents. The use of through bills of lading – the equivalent of air waybills, documents travelling with cargoes – is likely to increase in spite of the legal complications. Alternatives indeed exist in theory. Successful experiments have taken place with the telecommunication of facsimiles of shipping documents; the problems of such experiments, or of print-outs of documents at the ports of delivery are, once again, legal rather than technical in the sense that such facsimiles or print-outs are not as yet legally acceptable as originals.

If through-way documentation whether electronically or by conventional means is accepted as standard, the implications may be profound. At present a number of different parties from freight forwarders to insurance brokers have their own documents, and with such a multiplicity of sources of documents the dangers of a hold-up because one of a set is delayed, even by a few hours, grows. It is possible, even if only to secure speed and reliability in documentation, that one of the parties concerned may try to integrate the whole procedure: the first who can do so is likely to reap the benefits, and the most obvious candidate is probably the shipping line, in exactly the same way that airlines are already offering to customers many of the facilities conventionally offered by the shipping and forwarding agent. It may well be that in the not too distant future, the shipping or air line will be prepared to offer an all-in rate for door-to-door delivery, comprising not merely freight costs, but insurance and everything else. A number of the conventional parties to exporting, not least shipping and forwarding agents, may find their opportunities drastically reduced.

Finally, the conventional shipping line conferences may face a serious challenge. If the average shipping line with membership of a particular conference is operating general cargo ships as well as container or other specialised ships, it may not be particularly well placed to compete with the incomer operating only a few advanced-design container ships. Conversely the owner of such new and very expensive ships may seek to win the bulk of all trade in a particular conference route by undercutting the conference rates. In this sort of freight war the situation might not stabilise until the shipping lines with conventional general cargo ships had been driven from these routes.

In the long run the possible disappearance or merging of smaller shipping lines operating on traditional trade routes may operate to the disadvantage of the exporter by cutting competition. But the effect in the 1970s and 1980s at least is likely to be for speedier and more efficient services to become available, with the complications of a multiplicity of sources of documents becoming easier.

The price of these developments is likely to be that, willy-nilly, many exporters will be forced to discard their traditional approach to financing exports, including the conventional f.o.b. or c.i.f. clause; this would not necessarily be a bad thing. Whether the exporter is going to find the new facilities are in the long run cheaper than existing arrangements is an open question.

SUMMARY

The main point of this chapter is best summarised as that the older concepts of exports, f.o.b. or c.i.f., are rapidly being superseded by the possibility, indeed the desirability, of delivery door-to-door, i.e. the delivered price concept. In costing out new methods, however, it is misleading merely to compare the direct costs of the old with the new, e.g. sea freight charges *v.* air freight charges. Instead it is necessary to look at the whole package – to consider how a new method may affect stockholding and insurance requirements. It is increasingly important to remember that the next few years are likely to be a buyer's market for most products. It is the buyer's convenience, not the exporter's, which matters. Particularly in Western Europe and the inland markets of North America, this means door-to-door delivery, because that is what the domestic competitor will be offering.

Chapter 8

The Finance and Insurance of Exports

INTRODUCTION

Chapter 4 made the point that in a buyer's market, particularly in an inflationary situation, credit arrangements are as important as price. This chapter considers some of the problems of financing credit through banks or other financial instruments. The need to obtain credit facilities through the banking system implies collateral: an increasingly important form of this is credit insurance. Such credit insurance is the complement to marine insurance, but instead of covering physical risk, i.e. destruction, loss or damage to goods, it covers the commercial and political risk of foreign transactions. It reduces such risks to a measurable cost – again like marine insurance.

The system of credit insurance described here is the British system administered by a government agency, the Export Credit Guarantee Department. The same principles apply largely to the credit systems applied by other countries, e.g. the U.S. Foreign Credit Insurance Association system.

Finally, this chapter discusses methods of trading which do not involve financing by the exporter. A half-way stage is the use of factoring; a more complex and increasingly sophisticated method is that of barter techniques.

FINANCING INTERNATIONAL TRADE

Ideally, foreign trade would be conducted on a basis of cash on delivery, by a documentary letter of credit.

Any commercial bank will advise on letters of credit. Briefly, the best type of credit so far as the seller is concerned is irrevocable and confirmed. The term 'irrevocable' means that it cannot be cancelled unilaterally by the buyer; the term 'confirmed' means that a bank in the exporter's country has guaranteed payment provided that the exporter produces satisfactory details of delivery.

This type of finance involves one bank in the buyer's country and one in the seller's country being willing to accept agreed documents and pay out on them. The normal procedure is that the commercial banks concerned will have trading links, and possibly accounts with one other, being in a correspondent relationship. The buyer's bank will inform the correspondent bank in the seller's country of its readiness to meet drafts presented to it, on the terms agreed. On that basis the seller will be informed by means of a letter of credit that payment will be made against the presenting of specified documents – generally shipping documents – correctly filed. The letter of credit will indicate whether the credit is irrevocable and whether it has been confirmed. It is of course desirable that the letter of credit should be in the exporter's hands before the goods leave his control; preferably it should be available before any export expenses are incurred.

An alternative is cash against documents. Here, once again, the agreed documents are presented to the seller's bank with instructions that these are to be presented to the buyer's bank in the overseas country for payment there. The effect is much the same as by the ordinary letter of credit in that the seller's bank will not hand over the documents until it receives the agreed payment. The main difference is the delay in payment while the documents are sent to the buyer's country and any subsequent delay in transferring payment back.

There are alternative methods of payment which use bank facilities, but in general they are to be recommended only if the importer is well known to, and trusted by, the seller; the advice of the exporter's own bank should be sought on them. The main point which has to be kept in mind is that banks are likely to be even more cautious in affording payment against documents involving an overseas transaction than they would for an internal transaction, and the formalities have normally to be observed meticulously. Every document must be presented exactly as specified.

Sometimes it is impractical to secure payment on delivery, and the bill of exchange, or similar instrument, is then used in conjunction with an 'acceptance' letter of credit. The majority of these will be short-term credits – 90 or 180 days at most. The exporter's bank can advise on normal credit terms for a market.

EXPORT CREDIT INSURANCE

Risk has always been inherent in any marketing transaction and the risks have been particularly obvious in international trade. Measures to meet the situation go back a long way. Marine insurance goes back to the time of the Phoenicians. But the type of risk which has traditionally been covered has largely consisted of the physical risks peculiar to international trade and particularly sea trade.

There have always been other types of risk – of confiscation of goods, wars between the nations involved, credit failure and the like – and probably as many merchants were ruined in this way in ancient or medieval times as by the physical destruction of their goods. These risks, which might be regarded as political and commercial as opposed to the physical risks covered by conventional insurance, have been present since the beginning of overseas trade, but in some respects at least, the problems have increased particularly since the Second World War.

In the nineteenth century when the industrial and trading nations of the world underwent a tremendous expansion, their merchants had considerable protection in their overseas transactions. In trading with each other the same standards of commercial morality tended to be accepted by all. In trading with what would now be described as the underdeveloped world most of which was effectively under the control of the major European powers and the United States, diplomatic pressure at one extreme or gun boat diplomacy at the other ensured merchants' interest did not go by default. If trade followed the flag, the flag followed trade.

Whatever the merits or demerits of the system there is little doubt that the situation is vastly altered today. There are about 150 nation states in the world, many of them ludicrously non-viable in terms of economic or political power. Yet even the two super powers, America and Russia, would find it difficult to recover trade debts incurred by the weakest and least viable of such nations, partly because international sentiment has elevated independent nationalism at the expense of virtually every other consideration and partly because pressure by one superpower is likely to produce counter pressure by the others. If the superpowers have relatively limited success in bringing pressure to bear, the practical steps which can be taken by the government of a medium-sized power like Britain to protect its merchants are almost nil in many parts of the world.

The situation has in fact been developing since the First World War and Britain was one of the first nations to be aware of the changed circumstances as far as protecting the interests of her merchants was concerned. The result was the development, as early as the 1920s, of new forms of insurance not against the traditional physical risks but the political and commercial risks, namely export credit insurance.

There is no particular reason why these two categories of risk should not be treated separately; some national credit risk systems do so. In general, political risks can only be assessed by government organisations, while commercial risks can be treated as an ordinary actuarial problem susceptible to private insurance.

The British answer is a compromise: it is possible to take out insurance against political and commercial risk through a government-sponsored organisation, or commercial risk only, through a private organisation. It is not possible to secure cover against political risk only.

POLITICAL AND COMMERCIAL RISKS –
THE EXPORT CREDIT GUARANTEE DEPARTMENT

The great bulk of export credit insurance in Britain is supplied by the Export Credit Guarantee Department. E.C.G.D., as it is familiarly known, operates under the direction of the Secretary for Trade, and gives cover against political and commercial risks. In about fifty years of existence it has grown to the point where it is the largest credit insurance institution in the world, covering over one-third of British exports.

Basically, the principle in most E.C.G.D. policies is the ancient insurance principle of spreading the risk. A merchant who chooses to use the insurance policies offered will be expected to offer a wide range of export markets over a given period and not merely the particular market where he anticipates there may be difficulties in securing payment. The result of taking out such a policy is that, in the event of non-payment for a number of specified reasons, default in payment, insolvency of the buyer, currency blocking or restricting of import payments, war, civil war, or extra handling charges due to diversions of a voyage, the merchant may ultimately be compensated up to 90 per cent or 95 per cent of the costs. 100 per cent cover tends to be exceptional in E.C.G.D. policies, for it is a sound principle of business that the injured party retains an interest in the transaction rather than giving up all efforts to recover his losses.

What follows in the next few pages is a discussion of the general principles of E.C.G.D. policies. No attempt is made to detail the exact terms or interest charges quoted in the very numerous credit policies now available. These are, as might be expected, constantly being amended in the light of current political and commercial considerations in world trade.

The general structure of E.C.G.D. operations is determined by government legislation. The present 'enabling act' is from time to time supplemented by other legislation principally intended to increase the scope of the amount of capital involved in order to match the increase in exports, and inflation.

There are two sections to this legislation. The first section deals with transactions which are carried out on a commercial basis, i.e. the vast majority of situations where exporters have a fairly routine export situation with several markets, and where risks can be spread easily on an actuarial basis. The more business done, the lower, in general, premiums are likely to be.

The second section relates to credit guarantees in respect of national interest. This in effect covers large capital projects, e.g. the sale of large ships, aircraft, contracts to build factories overseas, etc. Here it is impossible to get a spread of insurance risks over several markets – a ship-builder is not likely to be simultaneously selling a dozen or more £10 million tankers in different markets, although it is clearly in the national interest to obtain overseas orders of this nature. Large or complex transactions of this nature have to be treated on an individual basis. The insurance premiums vary from country to country, but in essence depend on two factors: the terms of payment and the country or market concerned.

The terms of payment are in three categories varying from the safest situation of all – namely cash before delivery – to the situation where the buyer has possession before he pays, and has perhaps several months or even years, extended credit.

The assessment of markets is constantly under review, and decisions are based on credit ratings prepared on the spot together with Foreign Office assessment of political and economic conditions. There are four general categories, and countries are moved from one to the other as their political and economic conditions, as well as their relationship with Britain, varies.

Based on these two factors the premium rate is fixed.

The circumstances and costs of policies thus vary but it is generally true to say that, with the growth of E.C.G.D. activities and the absence of substantial E.C.G.D. losses, premiums have steadily declined to an average which is well below 1 per cent of value. Like any other insurance scheme operating on actuarial principles, it will regularly adjust its premiums up or down according to its losses or profits over the preceding period, so as to break even in the long run.

The principle of commercial and political insurance is not unique to Britain. Other trading nations operate such schemes either as a government service to industry or by private organisations with official backing. National systems differ in details but most principles in fact are fairly standard. The British system is probably as favourable to exporters as any, but there are a number of points which are not covered, and where in some cases at least, a foreign merchant may enjoy an advantage.

One problem arises from the question of exchange rates. E.C.G.D. does cover against currency restrictions, such as the blocking of sterling accounts, but does not provide for the situation where the currency of the buyer is devalued or substantially depreciated during the period of the transaction.

One answer would be to get a price designated in a reasonably secure currency; but in an age of increasing competition for foreign orders, it is often possible to secure an order only by quoting in the customer's currency. In recent years the British have been more concerned with the possibility of sterling depreciation or devaluation to note the very large numbers of currencies in Latin American and elsewhere which have performed even worse than sterling, and a British exporter allowing one or two years' credit on a sale made in one of these currencies could lose out badly through an event which was neither his fault nor indeed the fault of the buyer. What would cover the situation would be an exchange rate guarantee ensuring that the difference in the amounts received in payment in sterling would be made up if necessary by E.C.G.D. It is not beyond the bounds of possibility to envisage a 'two-way' option, whereby an exporter might, in part at least, exchange the gamble of a windfall through a devaluation of sterling, for cover against a loss through a devaluation of the other currency. At present the absence of any exchange rate guarantee leads to a 'leads and lags' situation. When a currency is under some threat of devaluation, one group of merchants frantically pays off accounts ahead of time to avoid the anticipated increased costs, while another group of merchants stalls off payments in the hope that devaluation will cut their bills.

Changes might be considered to cover more adequately the problem of the small exporter. Most of Britain's exports come from the larger firms; most of the smaller firms which could potentially export, either do not do so, or use other indirect means such as sales to export houses. If even a fraction of the potential exporters entered into this field, the British balance of payments problem would be greatly eased, and this suggests that there is a case for increased E.C.G.D. encouragement over and above the present arrangements.

A second method of encouraging the small exporter could

be the creation of small export groups – a method used more successfully by some continental countries than the United Kingdom. A joint export policy or a revolving credit which could be used by members of a group is worth experimentation.

There is a possibility of distinguishing between, for example, the economic and the political risk. In a limited sense, something like this is already done by E.C.G.D. in distinguishing between the categories of commercial insurance risk and 'national interest insurance'.

The American credit guarantee system, the Foreign Credit Insurance Association, goes part of the way to making a useful distinction in its guarantees. It offers the choice of comprehensive insurance very similar to the British system, or a policy covering political risks only. A similar choice should be possible to the British exporter.

Criticisms of the E.C.G.D. policy system do not disparage its obvious merits. The Department has to 'wash its face' in the sense that it must over the years break even, but it does not have to make a profit – a situation which is obviously of importance in some other national schemes where the policies are issued by private insurance organisations with government backing. The British scheme is more widespread in its operation than most others, and this tends to make the premiums at least as cheap as anywhere in the world. The more the system grows, the more likely are further reductions. The American F.C.I.A. scheme, although it has broken new ground in its selective risk system, in many other respects has been modelled on the British system and its insurance rates have not yet been able to match those of the E.C.G.D. system.

The E.C.G.D. is no substitute for care in assessing the risk. Certainly the insistence by E.C.G.D. that no information on specific insurance should be given to overseas buyers, illustrates the view of the Department in this matter.

The role of the E.C.G.D. is in some measure influenced by the existence of an international Credit Insurance Association known generally as the Berne Union. The Union, of which E.C.G.D. is a member, attempts to lay down rules on such matters as the duration of credit terms in order to prevent a credit war breaking out among trading nations. In practice the restriction on credit terms tends to become eroded as competition for overseas orders intensifies. E.C.G.D., like the other members, gives itself an escape clause in the form of 'matching credits', i.e. if a British exporter, tendering for a large capital project on which credit terms were as important as price, could establish that a foreign competitor was offering terms which far exceeded the conventional norm established by the Berne Union, then E.C.G.D. would match these terms. The difficulty is, of course, to establish the allegation of excessive credit terms by the competitor – an unsupported allegation will not suffice, and it is to be suspected that a fair number of 'gifts' change hands after a company gets an unofficial view of another competitor's tender; or that potential buyers seeking better credit terms make details available of those rival bids which offer the most generous credit terms.

There are, from time to time, allegations which are difficult to prove or disprove about evasion of credit insurance limitations on large scale capital exports. An example might be of a 'turn-key' operation whereby, for example, an industrial plant was to be built where certain credit terms came into effect once the plant was complete. It might then be possible to have the plant operated by the buyer, perhaps a year before it was officially handed over, because some non-essential finishing touches had to be made.

Commercial Credit Insurance Only

There are many situations when an exporter may feel that the political risks of exporting to a particular market are negligible but where he still wishes insurance against the normal commercial risk. An institution, such as the Trade Indemnity Co. Ltd, will provide such a service. In addition to being more selective in the type of risk, the exporter using these services may also be selective on his markets, i.e. he may be able to obtain insurance for all overseas business, or individual markets, customers or even single contracts.

It is unfortunately not possible to get world-wide insurance on this basis, but Western Europe, North America, and parts of the Commonwealth as well as Latin America are covered by this scheme.

Trade with Communist Countries

It is possible to take out credit insurance for both political and commercial risk for trade with most Communist countries through the Black Sea and Baltic General Insurance Company. Although this is a British registered company the majority of directors are, in fact, Russian nationals. It offers much the same type of service as the E.C.G.D. Documentation is relatively simple and each export contract is negotiated on an individual basis. It should be noted, however, that not all Communist countries are covered by this insurance company, but in general those which are on friendly terms with the Soviet Union are.

Stages of Credit

There are three stages at which credits are often required – before or during the early steps of manufacture, during shipment, and after delivery.

Credit during manufacture is a familiar practice, but where the type of production is so specialised that any repudiation of contract would result in the seller being left with unsaleable products and no easy means of remedy, then the banks or other credit organisations might hesitate to provide cover, unless the circumstances were such that an E.C.G.D. policy would be issued to cover the situation.

Credit during shipment involves two distinct risks – physical damage, and delay or harassment by political circumstances. Typical situations of the latter sort occurred when the Suez Canal was blocked by the crises of 1956 and 1967 and a number of ships carrying cargoes to Asia had to be diverted, with consequent loss of time and increase of charges.

Finally, there is credit after delivery which may be for a few months or as many years. Smaller items in the capital goods range may require the short-term credits applicable to consumer goods, i.e. up to 180 days and involving bills of exchange, etc. Longer-term credits may involve repayment by instalment and contracts have to conform closely to standards laid down by E.C.G.D. Examples are given below of these medium- and long-term credits.

Medium- and Long-Term Credits

Although most exports are sold for payment on presentation of documents or short-term credits, longer-term credits are necessary for certain types of capital goods. An ability to offer adequate financing arrangements is increasingly important in exporting, and the whole issue of supplying credit increasingly involves the problem of obtaining insurance to cover the inevitable credit risks. Before examining the stages of credit in detail, it is worth considering what provision can be made on this score.

Medium-Term Credits. 'Medium term' is defined for E.C.G.D. purposes as credit arrangements extending between two and five years: the intention of these policies is to enable the exporter to quote a fixed rate of interest on the credit terms regardless of what fluctuations may take place in interest rates during the period of credit. What, however, is that rate to be?

For years E.C.G.D. offered a 6 per cent rate, that figure presumably representing a rough average of what interest rates might be over the years. In the 1970s, however, inflation and therefore interest rates rose dramatically so that 6 per cent was not merely a bargain – it was an outright subsidy in that no bank would lend money on these terms unless compensated by the government for doing so.

E.C.G.D. did then raise its rates but not to anything like a market rate and the subsidy went on. This is not a situation which is likely to continue indefinitely. Firstly, there is little point in industrial nations subsidising exports competitively and expensively. Some set of ground rules, at least among members of the European Economic Community, would have to be re-established. Secondly, if the world-wide inflation of the middle 1970s continued, together with subsidised export finance, the ludicrous situation could arise where even in an industrial country, it would be almost invariably better to buy from a subsidised foreign supplier than a domestic one.

Credit guarantees in the medium range may be 'seller' or 'buyer' oriented, i.e. the banks are enabled to supply credit either to the exporter or his overseas customer. In longer-term credit arrangements, credits are generally extended to the customer.

Long-Term Credits. For the British exporter the prospects of financing long-term credits, i.e. for over five years, almost inevitably involve some sort of E.C.G.D. cover for the banks. There is no standard form of credit finance and a deal involves a four-sided discussion – the buyer, the seller, his bank and E.C.G.D., to achieve a formula which satisfies all parties.

The problem of longer-term credit facilities depends on two factors. The more general is the existence of 'ground rules' – for example, the Berne Union, which attempts to prevent excessive competition by long periods of credit. More specifically, the seller's government wishes to obtain foreign exchange in the near future, not in ten or twenty years' time. Moreover, commercial banks cannot risk becoming too illiquid because of credits which will not fall for repayment for years. By implication therefore, the Bank of England may now be called up to refinance credits for the commercial banks; by analogy the Bank of England has extended its 'lender of last resort' principle from discount houses to exporting. Increasing pressure from competing sellers is lengthening the period of credit terms, a situation which must cause unease to governments who are called on ultimately to guarantee the credits.

The arguments against subsidy in an inflationary situation are even greater in the long-term than in the medium-term. In long-term credit finance the loan is made, as has been noted, to the buyer although the seller is the party responsible for finding the credits and offering them as part of the deal. The seller may have rather less interest than he might in the fate of the loan, in that the bank, and ultimately the government, will have to foot the bill if anything goes wrong. This, however, is a situation implicit throughout the question of long-term loans where E.C.G.D., against its usual practice, gives 100 per cent loans. Presumably it can be argued that *caveat emptor* applies here – with the banks and E.C.G.D. being the sellers. If they are ready to accept the risk then the responsibility is theirs.

The whole principle of long-term financing on credit terms

is increasingly confused as more and more credit on longer and longer terms is extended, and the Berne Union's attempt to limit this becomes less effective. Any single government may feel unable to call a halt to the process and risk the loss of exports. And since we are considering the whole problem from the point of view of the exporter it is presumably up to him to make the best use of existing facilities, whatever doubts may sometimes exist on the general principles upon which official policy operates. In the last analysis the careful exporter can ensure that, if a loss is insured, the main burden does not fall on his own shoulders.

OTHER METHODS OF FINANCE AND INSURANCE

The commercial banking system represents the most extensive source of finance for exports. Other financial institutions also supply finance on occasions. The exact detail of these arrangements varies with the particular institution, but typical of the facilities which are available are those offered by British finance houses which have entered into reciprocal agreements with their equivalents in other countries.

Thus an exporter, who was accustomed to use the services of an industrial banker, might find through him a financial institution in the buyer's market which was willing to advance a credit to the buyer. There are a number of such international credit unions and, generally speaking, a finance house in this country may have membership of one such union, particularly in Europe or North America. These are often advertised in the financial press and are also listed in part in Department of Trade publications.

It is likely that the newcomer to exporting will find the more common methods of finance and insurance the more practical, unless domestic policies have resulted in already extensive use of the finance house which offer such services.

Finally, it is worth remembering that credit insurance is just that; it is not physical insurance. If there is any likelihood of claims or destruction of the goods once they have passed beyond the scope of marine insurance but have not yet been formally handed over, insurance cover for the ordinary risk should be taken out, at least as readily as it would be at home.

AN ALTERNATIVE TO CONVENTIONAL FINANCE AND INSURANCE – FACTORING

A little-used, but potentially important and growing method of financing, is the use of an export finance factoring organisation. Basically, such an organisation has branches in the seller's and buyer's countries, or some method of obtaining such facilities, and is often in association with local financial institutions which will enable it to collect debts. The seller will pursue the normal export activities up to the point where he has dispatched the goods, but will then forward the invoice to the factoring organisation and receive on the basis of the invoice either credits or actual cash. The agency, in honouring the invoice, will deduct perhaps $1\frac{1}{2}$ per cent–$2\frac{1}{2}$ per cent of the value, and so far as the original exporter is concerned, his interest in the transaction has ended. The overseas subsidiary of the factoring organisation then collects payment in due course from the buyer, in the usual manner as for a home sale in the buyer's country.

The main advantage in such a procedure lies in the fact that both buyer and seller are largely able to operate the transaction as though it were a local one, and pay or be paid in their own currency. What is really being bought is the saving of costs and trouble involved in creating an export organisation with accounting facilities to deal with instalment payments. Factoring organisations of this type fulfil something of the same role for the exporter of industrial equipment on credit as is performed by exporting houses or confirming houses for the smaller and marginal exporter in other fields, for the factoring organisation is selling knowledge, not so much of the foreign market as such, but of its financial structure.

If an exporter proposes to use such a factoring organisation, the procedure should be agreed from the outset with the organisation and with the prospective buyer, who will have to agree to pay the designated organisation in his own country.

The initial negotiations may therefore be somewhat more complicated than normal.

The factoring organisation will obviously take over some of the roles which would normally fall within the province of the seller's own financial department, possibly E.C.G.D., and certainly the commercial banks who would otherwise be involved in the extension of credit. Is the service provided worth while? It is difficult to give a universal answer, but there is at least a case for considering this facility; where the exporter is relatively new to the market and does not intend to establish himself on a more permanent basis there.

Factoring organisations, like those of export houses, tend to be limited to a number of markets where these organisations have knowledge of the financial conditions, and the facilities to arrange for payments to be received at the other end from the buyer. The fact that factoring arrangements have been used successfully in one market is no assurance that they can be contemplated elsewhere, at least using the same factoring organisations.

These organisations are a substitute for a firm creating its own export department, negotiating with the commercial banks in exporting, and with E.C.G.D. But the firm which intends to export overseas, markets rigorously and systematically, and may be advised, as in establishing channels of trade, to concentrate as much commercial 'know-how' as possible within its own organisation. As with some forms of trade channels, the factoring organisation can, on occasion, be regarded as a possible first step rather than a permanent facility.

There are other variations of factoring services, including collection facilities rather than an outright sale of the debt, but since facilities vary with the particular company, it is difficult to generalise. A number of commercial organisations involving, in some instances, merchant banking facilities, offer services in finance which can prove on occasion a substitute for the normal commercial banking facilities. The details and addresses of such organisations are readily obtainable from the standard publications of interest to exporters.

Factoring is a comparative newcomer to the British scene but has been longer established in other parts of the world, notably in the United States. Where domestic factoring arrangements are available as, for example, in the United States, it may be possible to use them. In general, however, these arrangements work best if the manufacturer is able to sell his goods through a selling subsidiary company he has established in the market, so that from the point of view of the factoring organisation the transaction is little different from domestic transactions.

BARTER DEALS IN EXPORTING

The continuance, indeed the growth, of barter in international trade is at first glance surprising; as an activity it sounds primitive. In its modern form, however, it is a highly sophisticated operation involving a gamble on fluctuations of commodity prices or a complex of trading deals to satisfy the requirements of many parties. It is not therefore the sort of operation to be handled by the relative newcomer to exporting.

There are two common barter situations: in trade with the foreign trade organisations of some Communist states; and in trade with underdeveloped countries with acute balance-of-payments problems.

Particularly in the latter situation it is very difficult to obtain any form of financial guarantee or credit insurance. Sometimes barter has become necessary because a country has simply run out of foreign exchange and may have defaulted on payments already.

Another problem which arises is that the commodity being offered to the exporter in payment may not be the type of product which he is used to handling. Some companies have found the problem occurring often enough for it to be worth while setting up a department to deal with such bartered commodities. It may be possible through such a department, or on an *ad hoc* basis, to dispose of the bartered goods on the appropriate commodity market. More often, however, it may be possible to use instead the services of a specialist in this form of 'switch trading', who may have to put together a deal involving several commodities before all parties end up with the commodity they require.

This form of barter deal is still comparatively rare in Britain, and so also are the specialists in it, either inside the companies or operating independently. But so long as the Communist countries and some of the world's raw material producers continue to suffer from a chronic shortage of convertible currencies, the role will continue to be important. The relative lack of expertise in Britain in the methods, as compared say with Holland or Switzerland, probably reflects the ambivalence of government attitude towards the practice; in the absence of a solution to many of the international economic problems, however, there is likely in the next few years to be a greater readiness to accept the methods. They may enable a businessman to exploit an otherwise unprofitable market in some part of the world provided he can get expert advice in disposing of the bartered products.

SUMMARY

For the comparative newcomer to exporting, conventional financial methods are best handled through the exporter's bank, supported if need be by export credit insurance.

Factoring is a specialist business confined to a few markets and most appropriate when the exporter has no adequate administrative procedures for receiving payment by instalment, or wishes to avoid tying up credit facilities by simply 'selling off' a future payment.

Barter is a growth area in foreign trade; it is however very easy for the newcomer to burn his fingers. Barter should be attempted only by companies which have facilities for disposing of counter-sale products, or ready access to markets where these can be sold easily.

Part III
Wider Aspects of International Marketing

At the beginning of the book it was noted that international marketing was a phrase with two distinct meanings, namely exporting in the orthodox sense, and comparative marketing. The final part of the book therefore deals with marketing and more general management issues when a company crosses the threshold from direct exporting to subsidiary manufacturing and marketing overseas. As has been implied in Chapter 2, long-term considerations may indicate that exporting by itself is only part of the answer, and that the distinction between domestic marketing and exporting, based on the proposition that the firm's manufacturing capacity is concentrated historically in one country, may have to disappear. The end result of exporting may be international manufacture and marketing, and ultimately global marketing where the distinction between domestic and overseas markets disappears.

Part III
Wider Aspects of
International Marketing

Chapter 9

Going International

INTRODUCTION

It might appear to be over-ambitious in a discussion of the problems of entering the export field, to consider in any detail the problems of the international company – the ultimate stage in the development of international marketing. But one must accept the probability that in the next few decades the role of international companies will develop enormously, and that a very large number of companies which are only vaguely aware of the opportunities and dangers which mass production and mass marketing are bringing, and which are only tentatively considering the prospect of exporting, may find that such a step will ultimately lead to international status, with production facilities being developed on an international basis. The choice may be this, or relative obscurity in a small and ill-protected home market.

The conditions which make a foreign market attractive to an exporter are, in many instances, precisely the conditions which will make local manufacture even more attractive. If it is the government policy in the market concerned to lessen their dependence on imports, then the company which is willing to co-operate with the intentions and ambitions of the host government is likely to supplant a competitor which is not.

Quite apart, too, from the fact that the international company may be the logical end of a successful marketing policy, there is often a more immediate reason for the potential exporter to examine some of the implications of the present tendency of the international company to grow in importance. The chief rival on an overseas market may well be a subsidiary of such a company, with all the strengths and weaknesses this implies. A subsidiary of an international company may be the prospective customer, and it is as well to find out whether this will have any relevance to his consumer behaviour – whether he is likely, for example, to purchase from another subsidiary as a matter of general company policy; or whether he may in time buy from a not-too-obvious source elsewhere, because of some reciprocal trading arrangements in the company structure. Going international will not give protection against such developments. But an awareness of the option of producing locally overseas on an international basis instead of merely exporting, may bring more awareness of the implications which can arise when one's trade rivals or customers are part of an international group.

The international company, in effect, represents the export of techniques and capital as opposed to goods. It spans continents, generations (expressed in degrees of sophistication and development), and even, in some instances, ideologies. The international company is not new. In a sense the massive British and continental investment throughout the remainder of the world in the nineteenth century was a form of such investment, and aggressive management in some of the smaller countries of Europe have led to their companies breaking out of the national mould when most manufacturers in Britain were content to exploit overseas markets by exporting goods rather than management. The expansion of British companies into the territories of the Empire, and later the Commonwealth, gave a stability and coherence to many of the political links between the members which proved a good deal more durable than the military or naval factors which have been eroded by the conditions of the latter half of the twentieth century; much the same can be said of the other European empires which grew up in the nineteenth century and declined in the twentieth, leaving an international company, in many instances, the most enduring link.

Nevertheless, the second half of the twentieth century has seen the creation of conditions which have given an entirely new significance to the concept of the international company, and it is these which must now be examined.

CONDITIONS LEADING TO THE CREATION OF
INTERNATIONAL COMPANIES

There are obviously a host of factors which play their part in the creation of conditions favourable to the emergence of international companies. The existence of long-established international companies suggests that many of these factors are not new. Nevertheless, it is profitable to look at some of the more recently developing factors before considering the traditional factors, because the vast expansion in recent years of the international company suggests that the newer factors are the most relevant. They are, in practice, not always easy to identify, although they may be deduced from an examination of recent developments in the international company.

The chief characteristic of the past three decades in the field of the international company has been the staggering growth of the American-based company. In the early stages, currency and tariff problems created by conditions in Europe in the early years after the Second World War played a role, but, even when the original *raison d'être* of the international impulse disappeared with currency convertibility and falling tariffs, the development of U.S.-dominated companies in post-war Europe accelerated.

The motivation for American companies to look outside their own frontiers has often been their very success at home. Conditions can be tough for the American company in its own home market, and this fact, combined with a suspicion that not only was technical know-how, but also an aggressive marketing instinct, less developed in other parts of the world, convinced a large number of firms that competition would be a good deal less severe overseas than at home. The initial successes of many of these companies had a salutary effect on local companies, but the incomers once established with ample finance, technical competency and prestige, could not easily be displaced.

A second factor which played its part in persuading American companies to go international was a shrewd assessment that it did not always pay to be too successful in the American domestic market. Success means growth, not only absolutely, but relatively, in terms of the market share, and this type of growth in market share beyond a certain point in the American scene creates a ready target for anti-trust legislation. It can be highly dangerous to approach anything resembling a monopoly position in the American market, and the successful company has a strong incentive, after a certain point, to concentrate on expanding its sales elsewhere, where the U.S. Federal Authority's writ does not run, where in any case that authority is less concerned with the company's activities, and where legislation on monopoly practices is less in evidence.

In the past decade or so, German and Japanese industry has proved to be at least as dynamic as American, but their companies have not 'gone international' to nearly the same extent as the Americans, although their home markets have been relatively smaller. One obvious reason, particularly in the case of German industry, may have been the loss of foreign assets in two world wars. In the post-war years, however, it would be interesting to establish whether the difference in behaviour owes anything to the traditionally greater tolerance of monopoly or cartel situations, as compared with the United States. It is likely, however, that German and Japanese companies will switch increasingly to manufacturing within their foreign markets, instead of merely exporting.

Most of the newer international companies, however, are still American – a response both to the resources available from the home market and the degree of technical development in that market, as compared with other parts of the world. What is particularly striking is that many of the new international operations have been set up within developed regions, i.e. in Europe, whereas the traditional pattern among the older established companies of British origins was to move into the less developed regions of the empire and commonwealth. Much of this movement still continues, limited by the increasing severity of measures against the export of capital from the United Kingdom.

Mention was made earlier of the role of currency and tariff problems in the immediate post-war years in helping to create opportunities for international development. Putting it bluntly, if a company had earned profits in Europe which it could not convert into dollars, a second-best choice was to use such blocked currencies to set up operations within the European country in the hope that, when convertibility did come, the money would not have been lying idle; more immediately, exports could be created which would earn dollars. Similarly, where tariffs or other restrictions on trade had been created to cut down the volume of imports, this created in the short run a readiness to contemplate local production.

Such steps by themselves were not likely to create long-term policies for going international. The operations thus created were likely to be stopgap, in the sense that conditions which gave rise to them indicated political and economic uncertainties which discouraged long-term investment in the area. But when these policies or their equivalents were re-examined after the political and economic uncertainties had largely disappeared (and general current convertibility did not come to Europe until 1959, years after the crisis had been surmounted), then there was a great incentive to continue. These conditions may be repeating themselves in other parts of the world. Pressure from the government of an importing nation to set up local manufacturing facilities, rather than supply exports, becomes difficult to resist; the more so when it becomes clear that the moment local production starts, either by a native company or the subsidiary of an international corporation, protection is likely to be afforded. Companies may in fact resist the pressures and blandishments indefinitely, if they are convinced that the market is simply not worth the investment, but a large number of companies find it expedient to co-operate with the inevitable and switch from exporting to local production. This type of pressure is most effective in developing, rather than the underdeveloped or truly developed, countries. It is the developing countries, or more particularly those which demonstrate that they are going to grow economically, and not collapse into political anarchy, Communism, or simple starvation, which have most to offer to the half-pressurised foreign company; and almost certainly most to gain themselves, immediately, from the development of new industry.

Curiously enough, the emergence in recent years of customs unions such as the European Economic Community, and the general lessening of restrictions on trade, have had some effects in encouraging the growth of international companies. This has arisen for two perhaps not entirely consistent reasons.

The first of these is simply that the prospects of a greatly enhanced marketing area, combined with an external tariff, makes it worth while for firms outside the region to set up plant inside. Much American investment in the United Kingdom in the 1960s was obviously planned on the expectation of eventual British membership of E.E.C., rather than on any optimism about growth within Britain itself.

The second is that although the most obvious results of falling tariffs has been to make exporting easier, it does not always follow that a tariff-free zone, consisting of countries with considerably different cultures, represents a single market. Especially on the consumer goods side, products have still to be designed for the national market, or even for a regional market, rather than a European market. The traffic in consumer goods, especially those with substantial transport costs, is likely to grow very much more slowly than the traffic in industrial goods or raw materials, and the effect of free trade is often to encourage companies within the international free trade area to set up trading operations via local subsidiaries, as much as to encourage greater trade over the borders in consumer goods. In many respects the main effects of these customs unions and free trade areas are likely to be the simplification of legal and capital export problems involved in the setting up of subsidiaries and even more important, in the creation of a new psychological attitude towards the prospective markets opened up by these developments.

Finally, one might look at some of the more traditional factors which encourage 'going international'. These might be summed up as integration – the desire by management to extend the field of its control into new regions. Traditionally, the type of internationalisation this has given rise to has been more often than not of the vertical variety; where a company, to secure either the essential raw materials of its activity or to secure a guaranteed market, extends the scope of its operations backwards or forwards – perhaps both. Thus, international oil companies in their heyday were active in all stages of the industry, from working the oil fields, to owning or financing retail outlets for the ultimate products; other companies owned plantations, mines, etc., as well as manufacturing and distribution facilities. These were obviously international companies in some senses of the word. But if they were directed almost exclusively to one single end-market, then they were not necessarily international companies in the most modern sense of operating in different markets using different manufacturing facilities. In many respects such companies were and are politically vulnerable. Their activities, in so far as they are confined to extracting raw materials as expeditiously as possible, may be seen by the countries at the beginning of the whole manufacturing and distribution chain, as exploiting their natural resources without bringing any permanent benefit in the form of new skills and industries. The fate of the oil companies which are steadily being pushed out of ownership of oil fields, is probably a forerunner of a similar loss of control by other extractive companies operating on an international basis.

The other form of integration, the horizontal variety, is of more recent growth and more obvious long-term benefit to the host nation. Horizontal integration occurs where a firm has developed expertise in a particular industry or process in its own country and seeks to exploit its technological advantages, not only in other industries than that in which it began, but also in different countries. These countries may, in practice, gain substantially by the importation of the most advanced skills and techniques developed elsewhere, with Research and Development (R & D) expenses already written off. Except where the international company which specialises in these processes threatens to choke off technological advance in the host country by the very completeness of the Research and Development facilities in the home area, this type of international company is likely to be welcomed. But even here, there may be a certain ambivalence at the prospect of loss of national control, such as is being experienced in the European countries whose computer and data processing industries are so heavily penetrated by American companies. Nevertheless, in spite of the reservations which may be felt by the host countries, the heavy R & D expenses, which have to be written off over a comparatively small home market, make 'going international' by a form of horizontal integration an interesting possibility for the technologically enterprising firm.

THE PROS AND CONS OF GOING INTERNATIONAL

Thus far, it has been taken for granted that the case for going international has in general been proved. There are obviously a considerable number of advantages, as well as disadvantages, and we must now look at some of these in more detail.

The first advantage has already been alluded to on several occasions, and might be summed up in the phrase 'general acceptability' by the host country. Faced with the choice of importing essential equipment or indeed any type of product, or having the same thing produced locally, most governments, unless they have considerable technological superiority and embarrassingly overfull employment, would prefer the latter. Certainly, any relatively backward or developing country keen to extend the technological base of its economy would be very anxious to see the growth of new industry.

Thus, from the point of view of increasing technical skill and, of course, saving foreign exchange in the form of imports, the acceptability of subsidiary plants as a substitute for imports can be assumed. But the argument can be pushed too far. Technical development is one thing; technological domination by foreign interests is another. Likewise, a government facing a foreign exchange problem would prefer to see the remittance of profits, rather than the entire cost of the products having to be met out of foreign exchange – especially when initially the subsidiary plant's creation may have meant a capital inflow. There are some financial qualifications which will be discussed later.

It is sometimes assumed that local production, rather than import, will be welcomed by the customer as well as by the host government. It would be more accurate to say that customers believe that local production will be beneficial to their interests, if only from the point of easier delivery and servicing; their general welcome for the principle of local production may wither under the threat of increased prices due to increased production costs.

The fact that the host government is often anxious to attract industries has a number of other advantages. It may be possible to get favourable treatment from the taxation point of view – if not a tax holiday, then fairly generous treatment in the form of investment allowances. Some governments will, in addition to what amounts to a tax subsidy, make substantial grants towards the cost of building plants in particular regions. One of the most obvious ways in which a host government may help the subsidiary company is by the imposition of trade restrictions on imports, once the new industry has been created: the argument here is that the first of the overseas suppliers which takes the decision to build a subsidiary, scoops the market at the expense of his rivals. The truth is a little more complex; more subtly it may appear that some of the advantages are at the expense of the local customers. Nevertheless, there is, on balance, the probability that any move to create a subsidiary will be followed by moves by the host government to offer protection to the newly created industry. As well as offering better opportunities in the host country, it is entirely possible that the subsidiary will have access to new markets, which have in the past been closed to exports or restricted on tariff or political grounds.

All of these advantages are of a general nature – they amount in a sense to the establishment of a favourable business environment. There are, however, specific advantages in the light of the relatively poor record of the British economy in recent years.

This is simply the advantage of spreading the interests of the company and so spreading the risk of boom and slump. British industry as a whole has been very much hampered by the erratic changes in policy of successive governments which has made consistent investment policy difficult and has, on occasion, produced remarkable fluctuations in profitability. Not all the national economies in the world are so subject to the degree of fluctuations of the British economy (though some are a good deal worse) and, in any event, there is a strong possibility that hard times in one market may be balanced by happier conditions in another part of the world. The international company, in short, is rather less vulnerable than the national company to the purely national slump.

There are obviously strong arguments in favour of the international company. However, the disadvantages can, on occasion, be fairly formidable.

The most general, as well perhaps as being the most potentially serious disadvantage is on the issue of conflict of interest. This can occur at least at three levels: conflict of interest at governmental level; between companies within the international organisation; and within the subsidiary companies.

Conflict at Government Level

The most serious example of conflict occurs where there is a notable difference in the political interests of the two nations involved. At its most extreme, one might envisage a state of war between two countries, within one of which a subsidiary company might find itself supplying products to be used against its 'home'. Less extreme, but possible, is the situation where a subsidiary company in a neutral country is more or less compelled by circumstances to trade with a country which is in a state of conflict with the company's home country. The extent to which a subsidiary can follow a directive from a parent company which runs counter to the political aims of its host country is likely to be limited, especially where the clash of interests between the two nations is acute. American-controlled subsidiaries in Canada and Europe in the past have been subject to a good deal of criticism for attempting to follow political directives from home, in trading with China or Cuba. There is little doubt, moreover, that British and American companies in South Africa supplied Rhodesia in spite of an officially endorsed embargo following U.D.I. Subsidiary companies in this sort of situation may have to plead *force majeure* if their marketing policy comes under criticism; but it may often be the case that the parent company which has an inkling that such a situation exists, but feels it cannot really stop without attracting a good deal of hostile publicity, may find it convenient at times not to enquire too closely into marketing policies adopted by, or forced on to, the subsidiary companies, especially if the clash of national interests falls short of an actual shooting war, and where the activities of the subsidiary may gain for it a share in a market which would otherwise remain closed to the parent company.

The conflict of interest at government level can occur at either end, with the home government or the host government. In a sense, the advantages from the foreign exchange point of view of the two governments can be stood on its head. Setting up a subsidiary means, from the point of view of the home government, that a steady source of foreign exchange for imports is being replaced initially by an outward flow of capital to finance the initial investment, and only later on by a reverse flow of profit remittances which will probably be a good deal less than the earnings from the exports which are being replaced. Home governments have, in many instances, considerable reservations about subsidiaries overseas, especially where an initial financial strain may be followed by unsought-for political commitments arising from the investments.

As well as possible strains with the home government, the international company may run into strains with the host government. The stresses of foreign investment and political implications have already been alluded to. Briefly, these may be described as the threat – real or imaginary – of 'neo-colonialism', with control of a substantial sector of the economy being in the hands of foreigners. This problem is expressed most noisily in the former colonial territories, who both desire and fear continued investment from their former masters; but it occurs also in some of the developed parts of the world where American investment has been on a large scale, and the occasional tactless diktat from the home office has received adverse publicity in the host country.

Other aspects of this conflict of interest with the host country are the form of industry envisaged. Often, the overseas investment is inspired less by the prospects of the local market than by the presence of desirable raw materials. In this situation, the international company is interested primarily in an extractive industry, where the processing will be carried on in the home country where the market exists. The host country is naturally enough concerned to ensure that the economic activities and technical skills involved are extended from extractive to processing industries, and a clash of interests can occur.

In the initial stages, as foreign capital flows in and import bills are cut, the advantages to the host government are obvious. But as time passes, and the memory of the substantial savings on imports fades, the host government, which faces a foreign exchange crisis, may be tempted to interfere with the remittance home of profits, especially if, as is likely to happen, expansion of the original investment is financed not from the home country with a welcome influx of foreign exchange but from local sources.

One of the happier ways of mitigating this situation is by the subsidiary company earning more than its keep in terms of foreign exchange, i.e. by exporting in turn itself. As the international company is by definition very much market oriented it is likely that the move from serving the local market only, to exporting, will come naturally; there is little doubt that criticism of the scale of American control of some sectors of industries in countries like Britain would be a good deal more severe if it were not patently obvious that the contribution of many of these companies to the foreign exchange earnings of the host country was considerable – above the average of the locally owned companies, in many instances.

These then are some of the possible sources of conflict at government level. What are the problems of conflict at company level, between headquarters and the subsidiary, or between different subsidiary companies?

Conflict Within the Organisation

The problems are basically those of devolution of control of policy decisions. A local company, naturally enough, sees the problem from its own point of view rather than from the global viewpoint of the headquarters. It may be to its advantage to expand the range of its products within its own market: it may see opportunities to develop markets elsewhere; it may in fact conduct its affairs as if it were an independent company nationally based and nationally owned, and then find that decisions which make sense in its own context are frustrated by policy decisions from headquarters. The more successful a company is in eliminating some of the disadvantages of its foreign origin, the more vulnerable it becomes to the possible conflict of interest between the various national subsidiaries who may be more ready to regard each other as rivals than as branches of the same company. Where this danger is potentially greatest is where the diktat of the headquarters company not only appears to run contrary to the interests of the subsidiary company, but also the host nation whose nationals are in effect running the local operation, and who may find their personal and national inspirations being frustrated by, for example, a decision to prohibit development locally in order to further the company's interests elsewhere.

Some conflicts of interest cannot be avoided if the headquarters company is going to retain any sort of control. But conflicts which arise because of uncertainty about overall company policy are virtually inexcusable. It may not be possible to spell out in exact detail the area of control which is left to the local subsidiary, but some consistency in policy is essential. If one subsidiary company can abrograte to itself more powers of policy decision than another, merely as a consequence of differing personalities in the management structure, the results can be confusion and virtual loss of control.

The problem of conflict of interest is likely to be compounded if ownership of the subsidiary is split between the international company and other local interests.

Conflict Within the Subsidiary Company

Finally, in the issue of conflict of interests, we have the problem of conflict within the company – not a situation unique to the international company, but more prevalent than in a national company. There are always likely to be tensions within any organisation, and the best interests of individuals rarely coincide with those of the companies for which they work. The obvious sources for such conflicts in the international company arise from promotion prospects, status and salary. Are the plum posts in the subsidiary reserved for nationals of the home country? Where they are not, are the key posts in the headquarters likely to be reserved for nationals of the home country? Has the headquarters company to send out an expert, even on a temporary basis, who is being paid at the home scale plus an overseas allowance, or at several times the salary of his local colleagues and the local national who is being trained to replace him? It may be realistic, indeed generous, in terms of local rates to pay the first local national only about a third of what the foreigner who set up the operation initially was paid – but human nature is not always realistic.

Apart from problems posed by the employment of different nationalities at different wage scales, there often exist problems which centre round the differences in attitudes towards types of work, status and salary inspirations, and the existence or absence of what has been conveniently, if slightly inaccurately, transferred from the historical or sociological concept of the 'protestant ethic' towards hard work and personal advancement. An exploration of some of the cultural implications in other parts of the world would occupy several volumes, but it may be summed up briefly in the idea that the more remote and unfamiliar the culture in which the subsidiary is to be set up, the greater the danger in taking it for granted that local managers or workers will think and act like their European or American counterparts.

The disadvantages thus listed have been grouped generally under the headings of conflicts of interest. One or two others may be alluded to briefly.

Other Disadvantages

The first of these is increase in risk, at least in the initial stage. It has been a theme of this book that there is a strong case for penetrating the distribution chain as far as possible, to ensure the control of pricing and product policy. Going international is virtually the ultimate stage. The converse of this advantage is that the more one is committed and so extended along the distribution chain, the harder it may be to pull out of a market without substantial loss. Pulling out by selling a profitable subsidiary is one thing; pulling out because the market has proved less attractive than estimated is another. Going international involves substantial preliminary overseas investment and expenditure of a virtually irrecoverable nature, and to go into an international commitment of this sort without very extensive preparation is likely to prove even more risky and disastrous than in the more orthodox type of international marketing.

Secondly, there is a risk in one's relationship to the existing overseas customer. The point has already been made that the customer who favours local production in theory, as a means of obtaining better service, does not always accept the fact that a new plant serving a relatively small market and enjoying tariff protection means almost certainly increased costs. A firm which goes international under the impression that its customers will approve in practice as well as in theory, may find that it becomes unpopular. Prices increase not only in that company's products but also in the rivals' which while still imported attract a higher tariff. It may sometimes pay not to be the first company to set up a subsidiary in a market but to wait until another overseas company has broken the ground and incurred the unpopularity of pushing prices up.

Finally, in listing some possible disadvantages, there is a problem already commented upon which can arise either in exporting or in local production, where the general level of technology and sophistication in the market is lower than in the home market. So far as product policy and the general problems of production are concerned, the problem may have been recognised, and a deliberate decision made to use less sophisticated methods and perhaps produce a lower quality product than would be acceptable at home. But some other problems, especially on the production side, may not have been anticipated, particularly on the issue of supplies and ancillary services. These may be available at home with perfect satisfaction in quality and delivery dates; but can the same always be said of the situation in the new market? If, for example, a decision has been made to use local sources of raw materials, local transportation facilities, etc., a number of important policy decisions may have been made on what can prove to be untenable assumptions. But it may happen that the general availability of ancillary services, components, etc., proves to be below standard. The company may be compelled to import from traditional home sources, and as a long-term solution move into local production in these fields itself. The result can be that the subsidiary company is both smaller in scale and less sophisticated as a production unit than the parent company, but at the same time become far more widely spread in its production facilities than had ever been envisaged.

FINANCIAL PROBLEMS

The greatest financial problem of going international is the raising of the necessary funds. Many firms in this situation find themselves using a mixture of transferred funds and locally raised capital and loans for everyday finance. A good mixture is one where fixed capital assets can be ascribed to the funds transferred from home or elsewhere overseas, while working capital has been raised locally.

This is only one solution – and it should be emphasised that it is a long-term solution; in the initial stages the bulk of finance is likely to come from the home country, unless the host country, for reasons of its own, intends to make loans, grants, or takes an equity share.

The arguments for starting with substantial funds transferred into the host country are obvious; unless the company has an international reputation already, it will be necessary to 'show willing' by putting up funds, before the project will be taken seriously or welcomed by the local financial institutions. The prospects of an unknown firm coming in from overseas with the announced intention of raising its funds locally (and incidentally abrogating control overseas), is not to be taken too seriously; the fact too, that the risk will be greatest in the early stages reinforces the argument that, initially at least, most of the capital, whether fixed or working, will have to be imported whichever long-term division in finance is being contemplated.

Even where capital equipment can be obtained locally it may be easier to arrange a capital transfer if as much equipment as possible is purchased at home and shipped out. In general, unless 'early, substantial, and continuing' benefits to the British balance of payments can be demonstrated to the satisfaction of the exchange control authorities, the problems of obtaining approval for capital transfers wil not be easy for a British manufacturer.

In some instances, however, British official policy can be used to promote such overseas enterprises. Although the tendency has been in the past for British loans – mainly to Commonwealth countries – to have relatively few strings attached, it appears likely that the tendency will be towards 'tied loans' which are in effect available to be spent only in the lender's country. Where overseas developments carry local government support it is possible to link such projects to these loans. So far as long-term financing is concerned, a long-term export credit based on a sale to an overseas subsidiary may qualify for E.C.G.D. approval and cover.

The prospects of tapping some of the financial sources in the United Kingdom will depend on the extent of the host government's interest in securing such a manufacturing company within its frontiers. But local host government approval may give rise to even more substantial local benefits, in the form of tax holidays, local subsidies, etc. One has merely to consider the extent of investment loan grants available even in a developed country like Britain to site new companies in approved regions, to realise that the opportunities for an overseas company to 'cash in' on these policies may be substantial. Many developing countries will give substantial aid to attract the right industries; the political strings which may be attached to these offers, however, require some examination. These may require local control, with the majority of directors being local nationals.

Whether the initial capital is imported or raised with local state help, the arrangements described are scarcely a permanent solution to the problem of finance and, at this stage, serious consideration must be given to raising local finance either to expand operations or to give a more satisfactory ratio of home and locally raised finance.

There are two obvious methods of raising capital through the local financial centres. These are through the issue of equity shares, or by the floating of loans, mortgages, debentures, etc.

There are advantages and disadvantages of local equity-holders, even where this is politically practical. The shareholders have a more direct interest, and their existence provides a powerful source of support should an element of anti-foreign feeling emerge. Against this, however, there is some danger of losing control if the majority of equity shares pass out of the control of the company. This is not a very likely result but it may happen that company policy will change, and a decision to recover complete control by buying back the shares can prove expensive. A more general danger is that an obvious conflict of interest between the international interests of the parent company and local shareholder's interests may attract unfavourable publicity.

In spite of the dangers, the prospects of raising local capital in this way in an underdeveloped country are good, for the implication of an international company thus establishing itself successfully is that it is at least as efficient as local industry and may well be recognised as a potential growth industry.

The second method of raising such capital is by offering a good return on loans, at a fixed rate, but with no element of control. Obviously, such methods avoid complications of possible clashes of interest (provided the investment dividend continues to be paid) but do not create the same local vested interest in the development of the company.

At this stage, the capital structure of the overseas company will have begun to assume some permanence. Dividend policy may not receive much publicity, but requires a good deal of thought.

At the extreme, two policies may be followed.

The first is to plough back profits and not to withdraw capital as fresh funds flow in. In time the company may become locally self-financing, and develop considerable assets. This may be the company policy at home as well. Obviously this makes the subsidiary company a very ripe plum indeed to be picked, and such a policy of restraint may be wise only in a stable economy, politically and economically, where devaluation or expropriation are negligible threats.

The other policy is the opposite, namely to extract everything as quickly as possible by remitting home dividends as large as the earnings-flow will permit, and to replace and repatriate home-raised capital as quickly as possible by a policy of local borrowing. Such a policy is a sound one in an unstable economy; on the other hand it is not likely to make the company particularly popular and this may precipitate the very crisis which is feared.

In many instances, state action may be taken by the host country to limit repatriation of funds without outright confiscation or blocking. The principle of such a policy might, for example, be to attempt to distinguish between the returns due to foreign-raised and locally-raised capital and permit the repatriation of the former only. In practice, any such distinction is likely to be purely arbitrary, but it has a certain appearance of reasonableness which may make opposition to such actions a little hard to justify with conviction.

Conflicts of interest of this sort are fortunately relatively rare. A company should decide at a very early stage whether it intends to 'break even' so far as return of home capital is concerned, by dividend or capital repatriation, as quickly as possible, at the risk of losing some local goodwill. The obvious point here is that the dividend policy for the overseas subsidiary need not be the same as for the home company. Dividend and capital repatriation policies may differ from subsidiary to subsidiary, depending on the economic and political situation as well as the legal requirements of the countries concerned.

There is little that need be added at this stage on the use of local banks, except to observe that interest rates may vary substantially from those in the home region, and that a higher local interest rate does not automatically mean that it is costlier to use their services. The higher interest rate, where it occurs, may reflect a less developed banking system. Often however, it may represent an inflationary situation, and an opinion on what constitutes an exorbitant rate of interest in an inflationary economy has to be based on different considerations than those which would matter in more stable conditions.

Finally, so far as financial problems are concerned, there exists a number of complications in respect of costs, price and taxation. A particularly sensitive issue may arise on the valuation of plant and machinery. If the plant is to be equipped with second- or third-hand machinery transferred from a company operation elsewhere, what valuation is to be adopted, especially if, as may happen, some form of loan or grant is being made by the host government to encourage the creation of new industry? The book valuation elsewhere may already be nominal, but the actual value considerable.

This is a once for all problem however, but there is a continuing problem where one subsidiary buys from or sells to the home company or another subsidiary. Some form of transfer pricing must be adopted, and the price or cost (depending on which end of the transaction one looks at) may be used as a device to evade financial controls by the host country. If, for example, capital controls exist, undervalued exports sent to the headquarters company transfer assets in spite of these controls. In the same way, under- or overvaluing exports from a subsidiary ensure that profits can be attributed to whatever area will attract least tax. It is true to say that many of the underdeveloped countries are acquiring an increasing sophistication in examining unusual transactions to determine ·whether such motives lie behind them. But while the fiscal machinery of many countries remains relatively primitive, the possibility of such transactions taking place, or the possibility of a company being falsely accused of such practices, cannot be lightly dismissed.

DEVOLUTION OF CONTROL

There are fashions in management theory on the extent to which one should centralise or decentralise operations, and clearly this is a very live issue in the international corporation. Basically this is an issue which, handled thoughtlessly, can give rise to conflict of interest at an international or intra-company level. Even with the best will in the world some conflicts cannot be smoothed away and have to be lived with. Some of these issues have been mentioned in passing: the need to persuade the personnel of one national company to accept a ruling that puts the interest of another subsidiary or the home company first; the restriction on what seems natural development and expansion either of product range or of markets; and, potentially the most dangerous, asking personnel to co-operate in activities which appear contrary to the interests of their own nation, either politically or financially.

Conflict can never be eliminated; but clear policy decisions on the issue of centralisation or decentralisation will help to avoid gratuitous conflict. It is impossible to be dogmatic about which policy decisions should be reserved for the home company and which should devolve down to the subsidiary. But it may be helpful to list the fields of policy decision or activities, in descending order of priority, which should be reserved to the home company. The first one or two are almost unarguably central office decisions, but the latter are more open to question in particular instances.

The first of these issues is the capital structure of the overseas companies. Any decision which will affect this structure and with it control of the subsidiary must be decided from the centre.

Less exceptionally, but almost as critical from the financial point of view, is the company budget for the coming year. The budget of the subsidiary company is not likely to be drawn up by the parent company. But the ultimate approval of the detailed plan ought to be with the home company, if only as a recognition of where the ultimate authority lies, and as a discipline for the subsidiary company.

Next, the appointment of the top personnel: at least the managing director or his equivalent will have to be appointed by the home company, and arguably many of the other key personnel in conjunction with the managing director. The test for deciding which appointments should be made or sanctioned by the home company would be whether they are 'sensitive' posts, i.e. those where the holder would have to know almost by instinct just when a problem involved such a level of policy making as to require clearance by the home office.

Finally, among the issues more distinctly involving reference to headquarters, one must list the allocation of market areas, both in the geographical and product range sense. It is not unknown for a multiproduct firm to permit, and indeed encourage, some competition between its lines. But there is no real case for allowing any such competition in the international arena through lack of definition of areas. In a period of falling tariff barriers, customs unions or free trade areas, and legislation following from this on the subject of restraint of

G*

trade, the issue is important but by no means simple in practice.

There remains a considerable variety of other issues on which the influence of the home company can be debated. Many of these have been at least alluded to in this or previous chapters – product range, pricing and advertising policy – and the decision obviously depends as much on the product as in the policy adopted by the company headquarters. Indeed, some of the decisions may be made as much on the current fashion towards centralisation or decentralisation as by any more fundamental verity. One criterion is worth stating. If the subsidiary companies are ever to be more than hewers of wood or drawers of water, they will have to be allowed a share of the more venturesome elements of the company make-up; by a share, controlled and allocated perhaps, but nevertheless a share, of such activities as research and development. For where a subsidiary company feels that it is having an influence on the direction in which the whole organisation is moving, it is likely to prove more enthusiastic about its own role therein.

THE END RESULT OF GOING INTERNATIONAL

Managerial decisions on marketing overseas, like any other management decisions, should be taken in the light of some attempt to appreciate the long-term consequences of the decisions to act or not to act in a particular way. For a number of firms a decision to do nothing about exporting may prove to be as significant for the future health of the company as a more positive decision. For many companies the logic of a successful export policy may ultimately lead to international status in operations, if not in size. It is impossible to envisage where ultimately such activities may lead, and it would be at the least premature to discuss in detail the fate of an international company in terms of one which is merely contemplating 'dipping a toe in the ocean of exporting'. Nevertheless, it is worth outlining some of the possible consequences; some of these may be desirable, others not, and the latter can at least be watched for. Basically, and this is a point which has constantly occurred in this book, many ill and some good consequences can ensue from a change in managerial policy which may not even have been consciously planned or even noticed at the time.

The first possibility is that a subsidiary company in an expanding market may, within a relatively short time, become more important than the parent. Sometimes this process may be actively encouraged by the parent company, and a number of firms which have found costs cheaper overseas have not only used the subsidiary company to open up a new market, but have in time closed down the production facilities of the parent company and used the latter merely as an importing agency for the original market. The change in the centre of gravity of the company may be deliberate, but it may reflect the dynamism of the new market. The process can be accelerated, as has been suggested, by policies, deliberate or otherwise, on how and where to raise new finance.

It should be emphasised that any such change of direction, perhaps, even of nationality, is not always from the smaller national economy to the larger. Labour costs, for example, may reverse the process in favour of the relatively less well developed country, as appears to be happening in the case of some American companies whose subsidiaries in Europe are now invading the American market.

A second possible development is that the subsidiary wins complete independence, not merely in policy formulation but in financial control. A surprising number of companies appear to have 'gone international' almost in a fit of absence of mind, and the very success of the overseas operation inspires almost as much apprehension as satisfaction; sometimes, much the same consequences follow when a change in top management brings in an individual whose main interests are in the home market and who is ready to neglect even a prosperous subsidiary overseas. In this sort of situation the tendency to local financing and policy decision-making, and the gradual alienation of interest and control, accelerated by government legislative and taxation policy, may lead to a situation where control will be more or less gracefully relinquished if a suitable financial arrangement is possible. 'Going international' has proved to be a blind alley not so much because the road does not exist as because management no longer has the will to seek alternative routes round obstacles.

The break-up of an international policy may be signalled not by a subsidiary achieving independence but by it being sold off either to a local, or a more aggressive international company. The sale of a subsidiary is not always a symptom of a turning back – it may represent a deliberate policy decision to concentrate in certain fields or products, but all too often it marks a retreat rather than a positive policy decision. It is almost invariably easier to get out of a market than to get back in.

Finally, a look at the success story of the firm which not only 'goes international' but goes beyond this to the stage when an international division in the headquarters is replaced by the multinational firm operating with equal facility in several or many national markets, and no longer regarding one of them as the 'home' market and the rest 'overseas' markets. The multinational firm obviously has restraints in terms of the practical size, and it is likely to take a generation or two for even an international company to achieve a global outlook. Nevertheless, in an era when there is a reasonable prospect, at least among the developed nations, of the ideal of national sovereignty being modified on the economic and conceivably too on the political side, the concept of the national or even the international firm, distinguishing between home and foreign markets, may have become irrelevant by the end of the twentieth century.

Useful Addresses and Further Reading

There are probably hundreds of potentially useful addresses for the prospective exporter. The most important are readily available from the B.O.T.B. *Export Handbook*. This handbook which is an essential reference source is revised annually. A businessman already possessing a copy should check that it is the most up-to-date version.

The address for copies is

The British Overseas Trade Board
1 Victoria Street
LONDON SW1H 0ET

The B.O.T.B., or more strictly, the Department of Trade, has other offices in London as well as branch offices in the main commercial centres. The most important is

The Export Services Division
Export House
50 Ludgate Hill
LONDON EC4M 7HU

Export House contains the Statistics and Market Intelligence Library: this holds nearly 90,000 volumes, together with trade directories covering 150 countries and trade catalogues of overseas manufacturers.

Another useful series published by the B.O.T.B. is *Hints to Businessmen visiting. . . .* These books are available for virtually any country and give details of local addresses, customs, holidays, etc. Like the *Export Handbook*, they are revised annually.

Two services are available on subscription from the Department of Trade:

(a) *Trade and Industry*, published weekly
(b) The Export Intelligence Service computerised 'card service' which supplies details of potential overseas customers: this has been described earlier.

Another useful source of export information is

> The National Economic Development Office
> Millbank Tower
> Millbank
> LONDON SW1P 4QX

The major importance of this source is twofold.

(a) The occasional publication on the mechanics of exporting such as those listed later.
(b) Reports on the problems of particular industries, by the 'Little Neddies'.

For exporters who are contemplating selling via export houses, buying houses, etc., details can be obtained from

> The British Export Houses Association
> 69 Cannon Street
> LONDON EC4N 5AB

For exporters who wish to export more actively, information on subsidised overseas tours and missions can be obtained from the B.O.T.B., chambers of commerce, etc.

Licensing: a brief description of the problems and advantages of licensing, as an alternative to exporting, is available from the B.O.T.B., *Export Know-How: a Guide to Overseas Licensing*.

Advertising and Promotion Overseas

Information on Trade Fairs is published regularly in *Trade and Industry*. Other useful advice can be sought from the Fairs and Promotions Branch of the Department of Trade at Export House.

Other useful addresses for advice on overseas promotional material

> The Central Office of Information
> Hercules Road
> Westminster Bridge Road
> LONDON SE1 7DU

> The External Services of the B.B.C.
> Bush House
> Strand
> LONDON WC2B 4PH

Advice on the Mechanics of Exporting and Documentation

The best source is
> The Institute of Freight Forwarders Ltd
> Suffield House
> 9 Paradise Road
> Richmond
> SURREY TW9 15A

Individual organisations advertise in *Trade and Industry* and other trade journals.

Containers Hire: There are now a number of container-hire organisations also advertising in trade journals, etc. In many instances they are owned jointly by shipping lines offering container services.

Papers such as *Lloyd's List and Shipping Gazette* give details of shipping services available.

Through Traffic: Air, Roll-on/Roll-off, and Lift-on/Lift-off: Relevant publications by the National Economic Development Council include

> *Through Transport to Europe*
> (H.M.S.O., 1967)
> *Follow-up Report on Through Transport to Europe*
> (H.M.S.O., 1968)
> *Exports by Air* (H.M.S.O., 1967)
> *Movement of Exports* (1969)

The Freight Forwarders (H.M.S.O., 1970)
No Waiting at the Docks (1972)

Details of the air services available are widely advertised by the airlines in the trade journals. Many of them publish pamphlets, literature, etc., which are sent on request.

See also *Freight Management*, published monthly by Temple Press Ltd.

Packaging: Export packers advertise in the same newspapers, journals, etc., as the other services mentioned here.

Useful addresses in this connection are

PIRA (i.e. the Research Association for the Paper and
　　Board, Printing and Packaging Industries)
Randalls Road
Leatherhead
SURREY KT22 7RU

A packaging code is published by

The British Standards Institution
Technical Help to Exporters Scheme
2 Park Street
LONDON W1A 2BS

Documentation

See *Simpler Export Documents*, originally published by the Board of Trade but now the responsibility of the Simplification of International Trade Procedures Board (SITPRO), 26/32 Caxton Street, London SW1H ORJ. Commercial organisations, etc., will supply private documents, invoices, etc. Official documents, e.g. Customs Declarations, Port Authority Forms, etc., are available from the appropriate departments; so too is advice on classification of goods on these documents for purposes of customs, etc.

See also publications of

The Institute of Export
World Trade Centre
LONDON E1 9AA

> The Institute of Marketing
> Moor Hall
> Cookham
> BERKS. SL6 9QH

Finance and Insurance

Virtually all the commercial banks, British and foreign, publish pamphlets, etc., giving details of their commercial services.

Details of E.C.G.D. services are available from

> E.C.G.D.
> Aldermanbury House
> Aldermanbury
> LONDON EC2P 2EL

or any of its branch offices. Since details are likely to be changed fairly often it is important to keep up to date on the latest E.C.G.D. information and pamphlets.

Commercial Insurance only can be dealt with, with the Trade Indemnity Co. Ltd, at 31–45 Gresham Street, London EC2V 7EE.

Other methods of finance and insurance can be found by application to hire-purchase organisations, etc. Details of current international credit union arrangements by these private means are also available in the B.O.T.B. *Export Handbook.*

Factoring and other services are likewise widely advertised in the relevant trade journals.

Further Reading

General Reference

> *Croner's Reference Book for Exporters* (loose-leaf, with an amendment service by subscription)
> *Exporter's Year Book: Syren and Shipping* (annual)
> C. MacMillan and S. Paulden: *Export Agents* (Gower Press, 1974)

A. W. Mason: *Export: a Manual of Instruction* (Business Books, 1973)

C. M. Schmittoff: *The Export Trade* (Stevens, 1969)

W. W. Syrett: *The Finance of Overseas Trade* (Pitman, 1971)

D. P. Whiting: *Finance of Foreign Trade* (Macdonald & Evans, 1968)

Legal procedures, documentation and official form numbers are liable to change, and most of the books listed above are updated regularly to take account of these changes. It is important therefore to use the latest editions, particularly where documentation procedures are being discussed.

Glossary

Berne Union. An international organisation of Export Credit Insurers, whether government- or commercially-sponsored, which attempts to lay down conditions to be observed by member nations in extending credit insurance. Current recommendations vary between a maximum of six months and a maximum of five years, depending on the nature of the goods which are being bought on credit.

Brussels Tariff Nomenclature. A system of classifying goods for tariff purposes, accepted as standard by the United Kingdom and many other governments. The principles of valuation of imports are intended to provide a rational and relatively simple standard treatment of imports. Originally the system was confined to members of the European Customs Union, but is now widely used elsewhere.

Comecon. The Council for Mutual Economic Aid has been loosely defined as the Communist Common Market. It is a trading bloc comprising East European Communist countries. Its practical effect, so far as the British exporter is concerned, is that it endeavours to limit imports into Eastern Europe from outside, to those items which cannot conveniently be produced inside.

Commonwealth Preference. A system of discriminatory tariffs intended to give mutual tariff concessions to members of the Commonwealth. Developed as Imperial Preference in the 1930s it was important in the immediate post-war years, when most of the nations practising the system also co-operated in currency controls. It declined rapidly in the 1950s and 1960s and was virtually ended by the accession of the United Kingdom to the European Economic Community.

Containerisation. A term used to cover the tendency in recent years to pack exports in returnable standard-sized metal containers which can be rented from container companies. The advantages are speed of movement, cheapness and security in that, ideally, a container loaded in the exporter's premises is not unloaded until its final delivery to the buyer. Containers can be carried on specially designed road vehicles, rail wagons and ships. Containerisation requires special loading and unloading facilities at either end of the sea journey and container ports are being developed rapidly throughout the United Kingdom and most other nations.

Convertibility. The term, used in respect of currencies such as sterling, has had a variety of meanings, but, as understood at present, means the freedom of the holder of one currency to change it into another. Many monetary authorities permit current convertibility, i.e. a foreigner who sells goods will be allowed to convert his earnings into his own or another currency; and a resident in the country will be allowed to import goods, etc., freely from overseas, converting his own currency to pay. But the authorities will not necessarily allow capital convertibility, i.e. the right to transfer capital funds abroad without control. This is, by and large, the present state of convertibility of sterling.

Deferred Rebate. See Shipping Conference.

Drawback. The repayment of tariff duties on goods and raw materials which are subsequently used for exports. The main problem of such schemes is to avoid an accusation of export subsidies in contravention of GATT. See also Export Rebate and Value-Added Tax.

Dumping. In general, selling below costs in the export market. Unfortunately it is very difficult to define when this occurs, although as a rule the sale of goods in the export market below the price in the home market (after allowing for taxes) could constitute a prima facie case of dumping. Most nations have anti-dumping provisions which can be invoked when a charge of dumping can be substantiated.

Export Rebate. A system of repayment to exporters of certain taxes which have been charged on raw materials, fuel, etc., used in the manufacture of exports. In practice it is impossible to assess rebates on individual products and the practice has been to fix a figure for goods falling into this category. Such schemes are liable to be criticised as being a concealed form of export subsidy contrary to the provisions of GATT (see below). The original British export rebate scheme of 1965 was criticised, particularly by the U.S. government, on these grounds.

Foreign Trade Organisation. Most Communist countries conduct overseas trade through such organisations under the general control of a Foreign Trade Ministry. They are responsible for both exports and imports in a particular industry. Generally these are the organisations with whom British exporters will have to deal with initially in Communist markets; one problem they may create is that the F.T.O.'s interests may not be exactly the same as the prospective buyer, and they may therefore, for purposes of their own, attempt to link a sale with some extraneous conditions such as payment in part or full by barter.

General Agreement on Tariffs and Trade (GATT). An organisation of more than seventy of the leading trading nations, for the purposes of reducing barriers to world trade, GATT works on a generalised application of the 'most-favoured-nation' clause (see below), i.e. any concession made by one member nation to another is applied to all members. GATT conferences meet every three to four years, and negotiations cover the next few years.

'Leads and Lags'. A phenomenon which occurs when a currency is under pressure and threatened with devaluation. The crisis may be increased by a change in the pattern of payments for exports and imports. Any importer in the country who is due to make a payment in another currency may prefer to do so ahead of the due date less he should incur extra costs by delay if his own currency is devalued: conversely any overseas buyer who is due to pay an account in the threatened currency will delay payment as long as possible, hoping that a devaluation will reduce the expenditure in his own currency.

Letter of Credit. A financial document issued by one bank generally to a correspondent bank instructing it to pay money to a third person, e.g. to an exporter who has shipped goods

and has documents which he can present to the bank to prove
it.

Liner Conference. See Shipping Conference.

Marketing Mix. A phrase used to describe the mixture of
factors which are important in marketing a product, e.g. product policy, price, advertising, distribution, etc. An assessment
of the marketing mix of a product may enable a marketing
strategy to be planned which makes the best use of the
strongest factors in any particular instance.

'Most-Favoured-Nation' Treatment. A system whereby any
tariff or similar concession made by one nation to another is
automatically extended to another nation which has a 'most-
favoured-nation' clause in a commercial treaty with the first
nation. GATT (see above) is an example of the generalised
application of this principle.

Open Account. In this situation an exporter merely presents
his accounts to the overseas buyer for payment at the agreed
time, without any preliminary documentary proof that the
terms of the export contract have been met. This is probably
the simplest method of export finance, but it is advisable only
where there is no danger of disagreement about whether the
terms of the contract have been met.

Palletisation. A system of transporting goods on a platform,
on which the goods remain throughout the journey. The
advantage of the platform (pallet) is that it can accommodate
mechanical handling methods (e.g. fork-lift trucks, etc.), thus
reducing handling costs. A pallet may be no more than two
strips of wood separated by two blocks, but more sophisticated
versions in cardboard, plastic, or metal, which may be
reusable, are also available.

Quotas. A system of limiting imports by fixing their permitted quantity or value in advance for a given period:
quantities in excess will either be banned or have to pay a
higher rate of duty. The main concern to the potential
exporter is likely to be how the quota is administered –
whether, for example, there is a historical national quota, a
national quota fixed by other means, 'first come, first served',

etc., since this will largely determine his marketing strategy to deal with the situation.

Shipping Conference. An organisation of shipping lines on regular, i.e. 'liner' routes, which meets regularly to agree freight rates, and thus limit the possibility of competitive price cutting. Shipping lines in such conferences often combine the system with deferred rebate schemes which, in general, offer rebates to regular shippers who are still using their services at the time of refund.

Tariff Duties. These are basically imposed for one of two reasons, or a mixture thereof: (a) for revenue purposes, or (b) for the protection of home industries. Revenue tariffs often apply mainly to high-value products though some less developed countries with a rather primitive fiscal machine may use them widely. Protective tariffs have the same purpose as quotas, and since they are signed to limit imports, may be most effective when they bring in least revenue. Tariffs may also be classified as (a) *ad valorem*, or (b) specific. *Ad valorem* implies that the tariff duty is related to the value of the import on landing. 'Specific' implies that the duty is the same regardless of the value of the individual product item. Compound tariffs are a mixture of the two. Tariffs may be discriminatory in that different rates apply to different countries.

Terms of Trade. The ratio of the price of imports (expressed as a percentage or index number of a base year) to the price of exports. Since U.K. imports are largely (but not wholly) food and raw materials, British terms of trade tend to move favourably if raw material prices fall, or at least rise more slowly than the price of manufacturers; and vice versa. The terms of trade particularly affect the prosperity of the poorer raw material exporting countries whose ability to pay for imports can be seriously impaired by a worsening in the terms of trade.

Value-Added Tax. A system largely sponsored by France but adopted by other Common Market countries, of basing taxation on the value added to a product at each stage of manufacture: the value added is in effect the sum of wages, profits, rent and depreciation. It has the advantage that identification of the various tax elements enables the fiscal authorities to repay these to exporters without contravening the terms of GATT. This tax caused criticism among nations not using the system and in particular the United States, where it is sometimes seen as a device for subsidising exports and penalising imports, even more heinous than British attempts at an Export Rebate Scheme.

Index